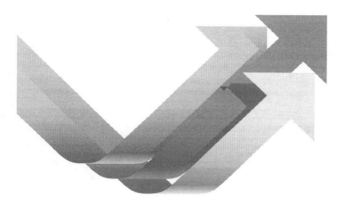

Mathematics in the Marketplace

An Interactive Discovery-Based **Math Unit** for High-Ability Learners

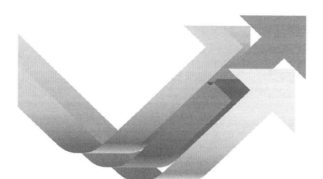

Grades 6-8

Mathematics in the Marketplace

Richard G. Cote & Darcy O. Blauvelt

PRUFROCK PRESS INC.
WACO, TEXAS

Prufrock Press Inc.
P.O. Box 8813
Waco, TX 76714-8813
Phone: (800) 998-2208
Fax: (800) 240-0333
http://www.prufrock.com

400635973

Table of Contents

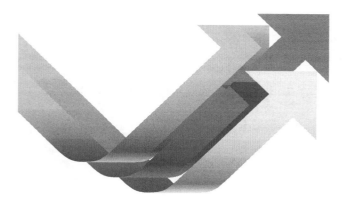

Introduction

Background

Gifted program directors, resource specialists, and—perhaps most importantly—general education classroom teachers who struggle with the challenge of providing appropriate services to students of high potential in the traditional classroom may be interested in these Interactive Discovery-Based Units for High-Ability Learners. The units encourage students to use nontraditional methods to demonstrate learning.

Any given curriculum is composed of two distinct, though not separate, entities: content and context. In every classroom environment, there are forces at work that define the content to be taught. These forces may take the form of high-stakes tests or local standards. But in these Interactive Discovery-Based Units for High-Ability Learners, the context of a traditional classroom is reconfigured so that students are provided with a platform from which to demonstrate academic performance and understanding that are not shown through traditional paper-and-pencil methods. This way, teachers go home smiling and students go home tired at the end of the school day.

C = C + C
Curriculum = Content + Context

In March of 2006, the Further Steps Forward Project (FSFP) was established and funded under the Jacob K. Javits Gifted and Talented Students Education Program legislation. The project had a two-fold, long-range mission:

- The first goal was to identify, develop, and test identification instruments specific to special populations of the gifted, focusing on the economically disadvantaged.
- The second goal was to create, deliver, and promote professional development focused on minority and underserved populations of the gifted, especially the economically disadvantaged.

The result was the Student Context Rubric (SCR), which is included in each of the series' eight units. The SCR, discussed in further depth in the Appendix, is a rubric that a teacher or specialist uses to evaluate a student in five areas: engagement, creativity, synthesis, interpersonal ability, and verbal communication. When used in conjunction with the units in this series, the SCR provides specialists with an excellent tool for identifying students of masked potential—students who are gifted but are not usually recognized—and it gives general education teachers the language necessary to advocate for these students when making recommendations for gifted and additional services. The SCR also provides any teacher with a tool for monitoring and better understanding student behaviors.

Using best practices from the field of gifted education as a backdrop, we viewed students through the lens of the following core beliefs as we developed each unit:

- instrumentation must be flexible in order to recognize a variety of potentials;
- curricula must exist that benefit all students while also making clear which students would benefit from additional services; and
- identification processes and services provided by gifted programming must be integral to the existing curriculum; general education teachers cannot view interventions and advocacy as optional.

These eight contextually grounded units, two in each of the four core content areas (language arts, social studies, math, and science), were developed to serve as platforms from which middle school students could strut their stuff, displaying their knowledge and learning in practical, fun contexts. Two of the units (*Ecopolis* and *What's Your Opinion?*) were awarded the prestigious National Association for Gifted Children (NAGC) Curriculum Award in 2009. Over the span of 3 years, we—and other general education teachers—taught all of the units multiple times to measure their effectiveness as educational vehicles and to facilitate dynamic professional development experiences.

The FSFP documented that in 11 of 12 cases piloted in the 2008–2009 school year, middle school students showed statistically significant academic gains. In particular, those students who were underperforming in the classroom showed great progress. Furthermore, there were statistically significant improvements in students' perceptions of their classroom environments in terms of innovation and involvement. Finally, the contextually grounded units in this series can be used as springboards for further study and projects, offering teachers opportunities for cross-disciplinary collaboration.

Administrators, teachers, and gifted specialists will gain from this series a better sense of how to develop and use contextualized units—not only in the regular education classroom, but also in gifted programming.

How to Use the Units

Every lesson in the units includes an introductory section listing the concepts covered, suggested materials, Grade-Level Expectations, and student objectives. This section also explains how the lesson is introduced, how students demonstrate recognition of the concepts, how they apply their knowledge, and how they solve related problems. The lesson plans provided, while thorough, also allow for differentiation and adaptation. Depending on how much introduction and review of the material students need, you may find that some lessons take more or less time than described. We have used these units in 50-minute class periods, but the subparts of the lesson—introducing the material, recognizing the concepts, applying knowledge, and solving a problem—allow for adaptability in terms of scheduling. The "Additional Notes" for each lesson provide further tips, flag potential problem areas, and offer suggestions for extending the lesson.

This series offers many contextual units from which to choose; however, we do not recommend using them exclusively. In our research, we have found that students who are constantly involved in contextual learning become immune to its benefits. We recommend, therefore, that you vary the delivery style of material across the school year. For most classes, spacing out three contextual units over the course of the year produces optimal results.

These units may be used in place of other curriculum. However, if you find that your students are stumbling over a specific skill as they progress through a unit, do not hesitate to take a day off from the unit and instead use direct instruction to teach that skill. This will help to ensure that students are successful as they move forward. It is necessary for students to be frustrated and challenged, as this frustration serves as the impetus of learning—yet they must not be so frustrated that they give up. Throughout the unit, you must find the delicate balance between providing challenges for your students and overwhelming them.

The Role of the Teacher

A contextual unit is a useful vehicle both for engaging your students and for assessing their abilities. As a teacher, your role changes in a contextual unit. Rather than being the driving force, you are the behind-the-scenes producer. The students are the drivers of this creative vehicle. If you are used to direct instruction methods of teaching, you will need to make a conscious choice not to run the show. Although this may feel a bit uncomfortable for you in the beginning, the rewards for your students will prove well worth the effort. As you become more comfortable with the process, you will find that this teaching method is conducive to heightening student engagement and learning while also allowing you to step back and observe your students at work.

Group Dynamics

Cooperation plays a key role in this unit. Small-group work is fraught with challenges for all of us. Creating groups that will be able to accomplish their objectives—groups whose members will fulfill their roles—takes some forethought. Keep in mind that sometimes the very act of working through any issues that arise may be the most powerful learning tool of all. Before beginning the unit, you should discuss with students the importance of working together and assigning tasks to ensure that work is distributed and completed fairly and equally.

Preparation and Pacing

Deciding on a timeline is very important as you plan the implementation of the unit. You know your students better than anyone else does. Some students may be more successful when they are immersed in the unit, running it every day for 3 weeks. Others would benefit from having some days off to get the most out of their experiences.

Every classroom is different. Students possess different sets of prior knowledge, learning strategies, and patterns. This means that as the teacher, you must make decisions about how much of the material you will introduce prior to the unit, whether you will provide occasional traditional instruction throughout the unit, how many days off you will give students, and how much your students will discover on their own throughout the course of the unit. For example, in this mathematics unit, students will learn and demonstrate the ability to use the four basic operations (addition, subtraction, multiplication, and division) while applying stock market principles. You may choose to teach these concepts prior to using the unit, and then use the unit to replace the several days of practice that usually follow. Another option is to use the unit without preteaching the content and math concepts, instead allowing the unit's activities to show which students already possess some content knowledge and which students are experiencing more difficulty. If you choose the second option, it is important to use the pretest carefully and cultivate an encouraging atmosphere. This book is not meant to provide exact instructions; in every lesson, there is wiggle room in terms of how you work alongside students to enable them to demonstrate learning.

Also, you should feel free to use materials other than those suggested. If there is a topic or source that is highly relevant for your students, then it might be worthwhile for you to compile research sites, articles, and other materials about the topic in order to provide your students a degree of real-world involvement.

Using these units is a bit like using a recipe in the kitchen. The first time you use one of the units, you may want to use it just as it is written. Each successive time you use it, however, you may choose to adjust the ratios and substitute ingredients to suit your own tastes. The more you personalize the units to your students' situations and preferences, the more engaged they will be—and the same goes for you as the teacher.

Grade-Level Expectations

All of our units are aligned with New Hampshire's Grade-Level Expectations. These state requirements are similar to many states' GLEs, and we hope that they will be useful for you. For each lesson, we have listed the applicable New Hampshire GLEs in a format that illustrates which learning objectives students are meeting by completing the given tasks.

Adaptability

"Organized chaos" is a phrase often used to describe a contextual classroom. The students are not sitting at their desks and quietly taking notes while the teacher delivers information verbally. A classroom full of students actively engaged in their learning and creatively solving real-world problems is messy, but highly productive. Every teacher has his or her own level of tolerance for this type of chaos, and you may find yourself needing days off occasionally. Organization is an essential ingredient for success in a contextual unit. For example, you will need a place in your classroom where students can access paperwork. It is important to think through timeframes and allow for regular debriefing sessions.

You will also want to develop a personalized method for keeping track of who is doing what. Some students will be engaged from the start, but others you will need to prod and encourage to become involved. This will be especially true if your students are unfamiliar with this type of contextual learning. There are always a few students who try to become invisible so that classmates will do their work for them. Others may be Tom Sawyers, demonstrating their interpersonal skills by persuading peers to complete their work. You will want to keep tabs on both of these types of students so that you can maximize individual student learning. Some teachers have students keep journals, others use daily exit card strategies, and others use checklists. Again, many aspects of how to use these units are up to you.

It is difficult, in a busy classroom, to collect detailed behavioral data about your students; but one advantage of contextual learning is that it is much easier to spend observation time in the classroom when you are not directly running the show! If you have the luxury of having an assistant or classroom visitor who can help you collect anecdotal data, then we recommend keeping some sort of log of student behavior. What has worked well for us has been to create a list of students' pictures, with a blank box next to each picture in which behaviors can be recorded.

Contextual units require the teacher to do a considerable amount of work prior to beginning the unit, but once you have put everything into place, the students take over and you can step back and observe as they work, solve problems, and learn.

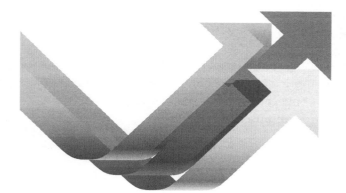

Unit Overview

These tasks and rubrics are designed to assess the degree to which students understand and apply mathematical concepts, such as estimation and rate of change, and perform operations involving percents, decimals, and fractions to make decisions about stock purchases and sales. This unit was originally designed in conjunction with the authentic performance assessment titled "Wall Street Decisions," developed by Dr. Tonya Moon, Dr. Carolyn Callahan, Dr. Catherine Brighton, and Dr. Carol Tomlinson under the auspices of the National Research Center on the Gifted and Talented.

This unit familiarizes students with the basics of investments before they run their own simulation of the stock market. Students play the roles of investors, bankers, and stockbrokers, using information about stocks and collaborating with their peers to make money. Students keep detailed records of their activities throughout the simulation, and after the simulation is over, they use these records to summarize, justify, and self-evaluate.

This unit is intended to challenge all students. As part of the role assignment process, you will want to consider students' scores on the pretest, students' maturity levels, and your knowledge of students' abilities. Participation will challenge students regardless of which roles they are assigned. For example, a high-ability student could excel as an investor, a banker, or a stockbroker. The investor is the "engine" of this interactive unit. The investor can rely on advice from his or her banker or broker in times of need. The banker is responsible for the bank's recordkeeping and that of his or her clients. The stockbroker is responsible for more diversified paperwork than the investor. Simply put, assigning student roles is as much a function of maturity, temperament, and cooperative spirit as it is a matter of mathematical ability.

Each lesson is subdivided to give you more latitude in differentiating based on students' prior knowledge, skills, levels of engagement, and readiness. It is left to you, as the teacher, to determine a starting point for each student.

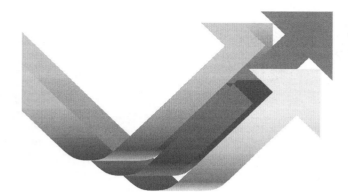

Unit Outline

We designed these lessons to be used during 50-minute class periods. Depending on the extent to which you need to review concepts with your students, and the amount of time you decide to devote to particular activities, some of these lessons may take fewer or more days than indicated. We have tried to note those lessons that will require additional class periods.

Lesson 1

An expert is brought in to present an overview of the stock market to the class or group. Various topics are covered: definitions of stocks and bonds; roles (bankers, investors, and stockbrokers); risk vs. return; calculating returns on investments (ROI); reading a stock market table; the importance of patterns; and how patterns are affected by current events. (Please note that this lesson merely introduces these concepts, which will be revisited throughout the unit and at your discretion.) A pre-test is administered, and the Stock Profile sheet is assigned as homework.

Lesson 2

The Living the Stock Market prompt sheet and the Interview Tips sheet are distributed. Students prepare for their interviews, which will help determine their roles in the unit.

Lesson 3

Students complete Activity A, Activity B, or Activity C, all of which require the application of basic concepts associated with stock market operations. An instructor or aide conducts these activities with the class while the teacher interviews students to inform role assignments. (If feasible, the teacher calls students out of the class to be interviewed.)

Lesson 4

Students are assigned roles as investors, bankers, and brokers, and tasks are delineated. All students have the opportunity to demonstrate an understanding of percentages. Investors must be able to make investment decisions and focus on their investments. Bankers need to handle multiple accounts using basic math concepts. Stockbrokers handle multiple investor accounts and track the changing stock market. Small-group tutorials are held regarding the particular paperwork associated with each job. (*Note:* This lesson requires 2 days.)

Lesson 5

Each investor begins with $10,000 on deposit with his or her assigned bank. Every day, the opening and closing stock prices and an issue of *The Wall Street Gazette* are posted. These provide insight into the future of stock prices. Students begin by calculating their gains and losses from the previous day. They are then given a set amount of time to "trade" through their stockbrokers. If they wish to purchase stocks, they must withdraw money from their bank accounts with which to finance their investments; alternatively, they may choose a safer return option by leaving their money in saving accounts. The final 10 minutes of each class are spent organizing the day's papers and tabulating investor transactions.

Each bank is credited with a $50,000 balance in addition to the money investors have on deposit in the bank. Bankers must calculate their investors' daily interest amounts and closing balances, as well as calculating the banks' accrued interest and daily balances. Money left in the banks overnight will accrue interest for each bank at the rate of 4%, paid to that bank by the federal government (the teacher). Investor deposits left in the banks overnight earn interest for investors at a rate of 2%.

Stockbrokers must be familiar with the stocks that are available for purchase and keep track of fluctuating prices. They help their assigned investors calculate stock purchases and sales, and they track the earned proceeds and losses. Five percent of any money that an investor puts toward stocks is given to that investor's stockbroker as his or her commission. It is up to the teacher's discretion whether or not stockbrokers and bankers are allowed to invest their own money (commissions and federal interest, respectively) in stocks.

At the conclusion of the 5-day stock market activity, students must summarize all of their work. This entails organizing the appropriate daily report records, checking the accuracy of the mathematical calculations that were performed, determining the amount of money made during the week, and computing returns on investment (ROI). (*Note:* This lesson requires 4–5 days.)

Lesson 6

Students are provided with investor, banker, and stockbroker rubrics according to their assigned roles. These rubrics will be used to assess each student as being "expert," "proficient," "emerging," or "incomplete." Two days are devoted to self-evaluation; during this time, each student builds a case that will show evidence of his or her accomplishments. It is recommended that graphs and other visuals be used. (*Note:* This lesson requires 3 days.)

Lesson 7

This lesson is for summative evaluation. Upon completing their preparations, students share their work using a fair or a class presentation model. The provided rubrics are used to assess student work. After reviewing both their own self-assessments and the teacher's assessments, students write reflections about what it was like being stockbrokers, bankers, and investors. (Forms are provided as prompts for the students.) The pretest is administered again, this time as a posttest.

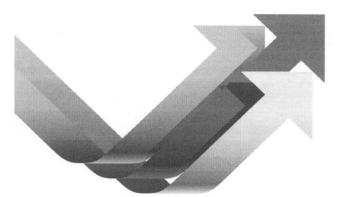

Glossary of Terms

For the purposes of this unit, the following definitions will be used:

- **Banker:** one who keeps money safe and provides additional financing
- **Bond:** partial ownership of a corporation, secured by that corporation's physical assets
- **Capital:** accumulated wealth used to generate income
- **Capital Gain:** the increase in value of an asset (such as a stock) between the time it is bought and the time it is sold
- **Equity:** a risk interest of ownership (stock) in a corporation
- **Interest:** the amount of money the bank pays to a customer, calculated as a percentage of the amount in that customer's account
- **Investor:** one who uses his or her own capital to maximize income
- **Money:** an accepted medium of exchange; a measure of value; a means of payment
- **Principal:** the amount of money saved or borrowed
- **Rate:** the percentage a bank pays (on accounts) or charges (for loans) its customers
- **Return:** the value or profit received as the result of making an investment
- **Return on Investment (ROI):** the percentage or amount of assets (money) earned as the result of making an investment; can be either positive or negative
- **Risk:** the possibility of incurring a loss
- **Stock:** unsecured partial ownership of a corporation; equity
- **Stockbroker:** somebody who assists investors in making investments
- **Term:** the length of time for which money is borrowed or loaned

Lesson 1

Concepts

- Return on investment (ROI)
- Reading stock market tables
- Stocks, bonds, and money
- Bankers' roles
- Stockbrokers' roles
- Investors' roles

Materials

- Stock market expert (presenter)
- Expert presenter outline (p. 17)
- Internet access/stock website
- Stock Market Pretest sheet (p. 18)
- Stock market pretest/posttest answer key (p. 20)
- Stock Profile sheet (p. 22)

Student Objective

The student demonstrates recognition of general concepts used in the stock market.

Introduction

The stock market expert uses visual aids to discuss the definition of a stock; the roles investors, bankers, and brokers play in the market; risk vs. return and calculating ROI; how to read a stock market table; and the impact that current events have on the historical performance of stocks.

Recognition

Students respond verbally to the presenter's questions.

Application

Students complete the pretest.

Problem Solving

Students choose a stock and complete the Stock Profile sheet. (This can be done in class if the Internet is available and convenient; otherwise, students can complete the sheet for homework or in the library.)

Grade-Level Expectations

The student:
- Demonstrates conceptual understanding of mathematical operations by adding and subtracting positive fractions and integers and multiplying and dividing fractions and decimals.
- Analyzes patterns, trends, or distributions in data in a variety of contexts by determining or using measures of central tendency or dispersion to analyze situations or solve problems.

Additional Notes

- You have several options when it comes to finding a stock market expert to present information to your class. First, you might contact a professional financial advisor. (In our experience, such advisors enjoy presenting to school groups.) You might also consider asking a fellow teacher who dabbles in the market to serve as the expert. Lastly, you can assign the topics to be covered to groups of students as a research assignment, and then have the groups present to the class.
- We suggest that the expert presenter take the class to the MSN Money website (http://money.msn.com) and walk students through the "Research Wizard" tool. (This is explained further in the presenter outline.) This way, students have a visual aid for understanding the process. You may use a different site if you prefer.
- If you schedule a presenter, then we recommend administering the pretest a day early; this way, the presenter's time is used effectively.
- To complete the Stock Profile sheet, students will need access to the Internet. If this is impossible or inconvenient, students could complete this sheet for homework or in the library.
- The students will complete the provided pretest as a posttest in Lesson 7, at the close of the unit. Because the same answer key will be used for the pretest and the posttest, we recommend recollecting the pretests.

EXPERT PRESENTER OUTLINE

A. Define the following, and describe the similarities and differences among them.
1. **Investors** use their own capital to maximize return.
2. **Bankers** keep money safe and provide additional financing.
3. **Stockbrokers** serve investors who are not risk-averse by buying and selling equities in an effort to maximize returns.

B. Discuss risk vs. reward. The greater the risk one takes in the stock market, the greater the possibility is that he or she will get a high return on that investment. The safer the capital is kept (for example, in a bank account), the less return can be expected, but there is a much greater assurance that the capital will be preserved, meaning that there is very little risk. Two illustrative examples will be discussed in the next item. The first shows a situation where the investor experienced a loss. The second shows a situation where the investor profited. In both cases—which are based on made-up companies—the results are rounded to the nearest percent.

C. Explain how to calculate ROI as a percentage.

EXAMPLE 1: SHS (ShoeStore, a trendy shoe manufacturing company)
Value today (12/1/10): = $1.36
Value at investment (12/3/09): = $45.74

$$\text{ROI} = \left(\frac{\text{Return} - \text{Investment}}{\text{Investment}} \right) \times 100$$

$$= \left(\frac{1.36 - 45.74}{45.74} \right) \times 100$$

$$= -97\%$$

EXAMPLE 2: ADV (Adventure Corp., an outdoor and camping equipment manufacturer)
Value today (12/1/10): = $30.88
Value at investment (12/3/09): = $24.97

$$\text{ROI} = \left(\frac{\text{Return} - \text{Investment}}{\text{Investment}} \right) \times 100$$

$$= \left(\frac{30.88 - 24.97}{24.97} \right) \times 100$$

$$= 24\%$$

D. Use http://money.msn.com to show students how to learn about companies' stock histories. Go to Investing (on the top options menu) and click stocks. This tool helps investors look at fundamentals, price history, price target, catalysts, and comparisons. If you prefer another site's content, you may use it instead.

Name:_____ Date: _____

STOCK MARKET PRETEST

Please complete the following multiple-choice questions to the best of your ability. This test is not for grade purposes, but rather is meant to match your interest and skill level with a suitable role in the upcoming stock market exercise.

1. A stock is:
    A. a type of racing car
    B. a share of a company
    C. a savings option at the bank
    D. make-believe money

2. A stock market table helps you to:
    A. calculate your earnings or losses on stock
    B. know how many shares of a company's stock were sold in a day
    C. use the stock ticker symbol for various companies
    D. all of the above

3. Which of the following statements is true when you are investing money?
    A. "The larger risk you take, the less you earn."
    B. "Risk has nothing to do with the amount you stand to earn from an investment."
    C. "The riskier the investment, the higher the gain if the risk is successful."
    D. "Safer investments yield the highest returns on your investment."

4. In calculating the return on your investment (ROI), you must:
    A. add the money you spent and the money you earned (ROI = R + I)
    B. divide your investment by your return (ROI = I / R)
    C. subtract your investment from your return and divide by the investment (ROI = (R – I) / I)
    D. add your investment to your return and divide by 52 (ROI = (I + R) / 52)

5. In order to convert your ROI to a percentage, you must:
    A. multiply by 100
    B. add 1/100
    C. divide by 10
    D. add 100

Mathematics in the Marketplace © Prufrock Press Inc.

Name:_____ Date: _____

6. How would you rate yourself in terms of risk taking?
    A. I am very comfortable taking risks.
    B. Sometimes I take risks.
    C. It makes me very nervous to take risks.
    D. I avoid taking risks at all costs.

7. If you buy 10 shares at $20 a share, and you have $208 at the end of the week, then what was the return on your investment? State it as a percentage. Please show your work!

8. If you deposit $400 in the bank in a saving account that yields 5% interest a year, how much will your account have earned after 12 months? Please show your work!

Please do not write below this line.

Assigned role:

Banker   **Investor**   **Stockbroker**

STOCK MARKET PRETEST/ POSTTEST ANSWER KEY

1. A stock is:
   A. a type of racing car
   B. a share of a company
   C. a savings option at the bank
   D. make-believe money

2. A stock market table helps you to:
   A. calculate your earnings or losses on stock
   B. know how many shares of a company's stock were sold in a day
   C. use the stock ticker symbol for various companies
   D. all of the above

3. Which of the following statements is true when you are investing money?
   A. "The larger risk you take, the less you earn."
   B. "Risk has nothing to do with the amount you stand to earn from an investment."
   C. "The riskier the investment, the higher the gain if the risk is successful."
   D. "Safer investments yield the highest returns on your investment."

4. In calculating the return on your investment (ROI), you must:
   A. add the money you spent and the money you earned (ROI = R + I)
   B. divide your investment by your return (ROI = I / R)
   C. subtract your investment from your return and divide by the investment (ROI = (R − I) / I)
   D. add your investment to your return and divide by 52 (ROI = (I + R) / 52)

5. In order to convert your ROI to a percentage, you must:
   A. multiply by 100
   B. add 1/100
   C. divide by 10
   D. add 100

6. How would you rate yourself in terms of risk taking?
    A. I am very comfortable taking risks.
    B. Sometimes I take risks.
    C. It makes me very nervous to take risks.
    D. I avoid taking risks at all costs.

Answers will vary.

7. If you buy 10 shares at $20 a share, and you have $208 at the end of the week, then what was the return on your investment? State it as a percentage. Please show your work!

$$= \frac{208-200}{200}$$

$$= \frac{8}{200}$$

$$= .04 \times 100$$

$$= \boxed{4}$$

The return on your investment was 4%.

8. If you deposit $400 in the bank in a saving account that yields 5% interest a year, how much will your account have earned after 12 months? Please show your work!

$$P \times R \times T = I$$

$$400 \times .05 \times 1 = I$$

$$400 \times .05 \times 1 = 20$$

$$\boxed{20}$$

Your account will have earned $20 after 12 months.

Name:_____ Date: _____

STOCK PROFILE

Step 1: Choose a stock to investigate. (For example, you might choose to research Dell, Coca Cola, or Apple.)

Step 2: Using the Internet, research your stock and fill in the following profile.

Stock name: _____

Stock symbol: _____

Industry: _____

Market exchange: _____

Last trade price: _____

Change in price for today: _____

Volume of trade: _____

Do you think this stock will go up or down tomorrow? Why?

_____

_____

_____

_____

_____

Lesson 2

Concepts
- Investors' roles
- Bankers' roles
- Stockbrokers' roles

Materials
- Living the Stock Market sheet (p. 26)
- Interview Tips sheet (p. 27)

Student Objective
The student demonstrates an understanding of the roles of investor, banker, and stockbroker by successfully completing an outline of the tasks associated with each role.

Introduction
After reviewing the material covered by the expert presenter, reintroduce the three roles (investor, banker, and stockbroker). Distribute the Living the Stock Market sheet, which will help students to understand the roles and decide which they would most like to play.

Recognition
Students should discuss the nature of each role with a partner. You might choose to have partners submit paragraphs to show their discussion points. As an alternative, you can have a large-group discussion and list the groups' points on the board.

Application

Each student writes a paragraph titled "Why I Want to Be an Investor/Banker/Stockbroker!"

1. Students should try to incorporate as much concrete reasoning and information as they can into their persuasive paragraphs.
2. They should discuss tasks they would find exciting and fun, as well as tasks they expect would entail a lot of responsibility.
3. They should include discussions of how they would be successful.

Problem Solving

Have students develop and write their own rags-to-riches stories.

1. Each student should create a hypothetical investor.
2. The student should create a company or investment opportunity and explain it.
3. The student should outline the investment decisions that the story's hero made that led to great success.
4. The student should attempt to back up the story with appropriate proof, terms, and logic.

Grade-Level Expectations

The student:

- Uses problem-solving strategies to investigate and understand increasingly complex mathematical content.
- Uses problem-solving strategies appropriately and effectively for a given situation.
- Determines, collects, and organizes the relevant information needed to solve real-world problems.
- Reflects on solutions and the problem-solving processes required for a given situation and refines strategies as needed.

Additional Notes

- This lesson makes the day essentially devoted to student work. You should begin by leading a discussion of the material covered in Lesson 1. After this, you can measure student understanding by collecting and reviewing the Application paragraphs, along with the rags-to-riches stories.
- If you choose to allow stockbrokers and bankers to invest, then explain the rules to students when you distribute the Living the Stock Market sheet. (Stockbrokers can invest with their 5% commissions, and bankers can invest portions of the money that banks are paid by the federal government at your discretion.)

24 MATHEMATICS IN THE MARKETPLACE

- Leave a few minutes at the end of class to distribute the Interview Tips sheet to students and inform them that their upcoming interviews—along with their pretests and written responses—will help determine their roles in the simulation.
- If you wish to use this unit as a cross-disciplinary study, you might consider using *The Westing Game* by Ellen Raskin as a companion novel.

LIVING THE STOCK MARKET

This week, you will be interviewed for a job either with a brokerage house, with a bank, or as a private investor. During the course of this unit, you will be given a chance to make as much money as possible. Documenting all of your transactions will be essential. There are many pitfalls on the financial path. Keep your wits about you!

Each private **investor** will be given $10,000 to invest as he or she sees fit. As an investor, you must be able to see the whole picture. Weighing the risk of an investment against its rate of return is a tricky job. If you leave your money in the bank, it will be safe, but it may not earn as much as riskier ventures into the stock market would. It is quite a dilemma!

If a bank hires you, your job as a **banker** will involve managing your clients' money and encouraging them to allow the bank to keep their money safe. Each bank will begin with $50,000 in addition to the $10,000 initially on deposit by each of its clients. This will allow banks to lend money to investors. Your earnings are based on a percentage of the money left in the bank each night. How will you balance the bank's desire to keep the money with the customers' need to earn higher returns on their cash? Your customers will deposit all of their earnings at the end, so if they make good investments, everyone profits, but if they make poor choices, the bank will share their misfortune.

If you are hired as a **stockbroker** for a brokerage house, you will have to be very convincing about your expertise. Your job requires you to gain your customers' confidence by recommending the right stocks for them to buy as well as when to sell! You earn 5% of the amount your clients choose to invest in stocks; this is called your commission.

Welcome to the world of high finance, and good luck!

INTERVIEW TIPS

You will soon be asked to interview privately with the teacher. This will help the teacher to assign you to a role for the rest of the unit. This is the first of many interviews you will attend in your life. Interview skills are very important to learn. Here are a few tips to help you along the way.

Do Your Homework

Preparation always creates confidence. An important thing to remember when interviewing is to be well prepared. In this case, you have to consider what the different roles are and what you would bring to each one.

Remember Presentation

Keep in mind that you never get a second chance to make your first impression. Presentation plays an important role while making that impression. Display confidence through your posture, dress, walk, energy, and eye contact. Shake hands firmly, but only if a hand is offered to you first. Let the interviewer start the dialogue.

Be Yourself

Relax and be yourself. Be honest with every question.

Listen

Listening is a very important part of an interview. Do not interrupt the interviewer. Listen carefully to what he or she is asking. If you feel that the question is unclear, then ask for clarification. Always be positive!

Lesson 3

Concepts

- Bankers' roles
- Stockbrokers' roles
- Investors' roles
- Risk vs. reward
- Risk vs. return
- Calculating interest
- Interview techniques

Materials

- Interview Signups sheet (p. 32)
- Interview questions (p. 33)
- Suggested role ratios chart (p. 35)
- Monthly Market Report sheet (p. 36)
- Activity A sheet (p. 37)
- Activity B sheet (p. 38)
- Activity C sheet (p. 39)
- Answer key (p. 40)

Student Objective

The student demonstrates an understanding of the roles people play in the stock market.

Introduction

Review the three roles by going over the Living the Stock Market sheet from Lesson 2.

Recognition

Students use what they have learned from the Interview Tips sheet to prepare for interviews for roles. You might choose to have students practice in pairs.

Application

Students check the interview schedule that the teacher has posted and attend their interviews as scheduled.

1. The teacher uses the provided interview form to standardize interviews.
2. While interviews are being conducted, students work on either Activity A, Activity B, or Activity C, depending on their skill and knowledge levels. (C is the most advanced, B is of medium difficulty, and A is the least difficult.)
3. Students can either select which activity they would like to complete, or the activities can be assigned.

Problem Solving

Each student completes one of the three (A, B, or C) tiered problem-solving activities as interviews are being held.

Grade-Level Expectations

The student:

*   Organizes and displays data using tables, line graphs, or stem-and-leaf plots to answer questions related to the data, to analyze the data, to formulate or justify conclusions, to make predictions, or to solve problems.
*   Analyzes patterns, trends, or distributions in data in a variety of contexts by determining or using measures of central tendency or dispersion to analyze situations or solve problems.
*   Demonstrates conceptual understanding of mathematical operations by adding and subtracting positive fractions and integers and multiplying and dividing fractions and decimals.
*   Recognizes, explores, and develops mathematical connections and is able to connect new mathematical ideas to those already studied in order to build upon them.
*   Understands that many real-world applications require an understanding of mathematical operations.

Additional Notes

*   It is very helpful to have a second person assist you during this lesson, as you will be conducting interviews and will be unable to supervise the rest of the class. If you do not have a teacher's aide, consider asking a gifted resource

specialist, an administrator (who can use the opportunity to meet students and perhaps perform a teaching evaluation), a paraprofessional, or a fellow teacher to help you. If you cannot find somebody to help, or if you prefer, you can simply hold interviews in class as the rest of the students work on the provided activities. It is our experience, however, that students are much less nervous when they are not worrying about their classmates overhearing their responses.

- Casting the students in their marketplace roles is one of the most crucial decisions you will make in this unit, because students must be comfortable and successful in their roles for the simulation to run properly. Carefully consider the feedback you receive from the pretest and the interviews, along with your personal knowledge of students' strengths and weaknesses, to determine which roles to assign students. The interview form has space for you to take notes on students' responses. After you decide how to assign students, you may circle their assignments on their pretests and return them, or you may inform them of the role assignments in a different way. You must consider the complexity and stressors associated with each position, as well as the social skills required to perform well in each position. For students to be bankers and stockbrokers, strong math skills are necessary, as students in these roles will be handling other people's accounts as well as their own documents; however, social skills are also very important. If you are afraid that a certain student will be hesitant to interact with his or her peers, then you should consider whether the role of banker or stockbroker might be too stressful for that student.
- While interpreting students' interviews, consider the following:
  o the level of confidence the student displayed;
  o whether the student dressed the part, acted the part, researched the responsibilities associated with the part, and made eye contact when responding; and
  o whether the student simply answered questions, or whether he or she brought up new material and displayed interest.

  If the student seemed confident that he or she would succeed in a certain role, did research regarding this role, and seemed capable of performing in this role, then you likely will wish to honor that student's preference. Make the best role assignments you can, given the students' preferences and abilities and the number of spaces available.
- Consider your classroom arrangement; desks should be arranged to facilitate students' work in teams and to provide easy access for investors.
- Help ensure the students' success by not overloading their caseloads of customers. Banks and brokerage houses should have pairs of students, a banker

and a broker, working as teams. Banks and brokerage houses can usually handle up to six customers. See the included chart of suggested role ratios, provided in the materials for this lesson, for more information about role assignment.

- Bankers and brokers may wish to invest their own money in the market; it is up to your discretion whether to allow this, what limits to set, and so on.
- On the Monthly Market Report sheet (and the accompanying activity sheets), bonds are mentioned. It is up to your discretion how detailed you want your discussion of bonds to be. The definition provided in the glossary, along with an example of how to calculate bonds at a rate of 5%, should be sufficient.

INTERVIEW SIGNUPS

	Name	Time
1.	_____	_____
2.	_____	_____
3.	_____	_____
4.	_____	_____
5.	_____	_____
6.	_____	_____
7.	_____	_____
8.	_____	_____
9.	_____	_____
10.	_____	_____
11.	_____	_____
12.	_____	_____
13.	_____	_____
14.	_____	_____
15.	_____	_____
16.	_____	_____
17.	_____	_____
18.	_____	_____
19.	_____	_____
20.	_____	_____

Student: _____ Date: _____

INTERVIEW QUESTIONS

Please answer the following questions.

1. What are some words that come to mind when you hear the phrase "stock market"? Provide specifics, please.

    _____

    _____

    _____

    _____

2. Do you think it is better to keep your money in the bank, or in a higher risk opportunity such as the stock market?

    _____

    _____

    _____

    _____

3. How would you rate your abilities in basic math? Do you find multiplication and division challenging? Do you understand those operations completely?

    _____

    _____

    _____

    _____

4. How well have you understood percentages and decimals? Do you need more help? Do you understand those concepts clearly?

    _____

    _____

    _____

    _____

5. Would you describe yourself as a risk taker?

_____

_____

_____

_____

6. Are you a well-organized person?

_____

_____

_____

_____

7. Which role in this unit (out of investor, banker, and stockbroker) do you think is most appropriate for you?

_____

_____

_____

_____

Thank you for your time.

Additional notes: _____

_____

_____

_____

_____

_____

_____

_____

SUGGESTED ROLE RATIOS

Bank A	Brokerage House A	Bank B	Brokerage House B
2 bankers	2 stockbrokers	2 bankers	2 stockbrokers
6 investors		6 investors	

Please note that these recommendations are for a class of 20 students. If you have more or fewer students in your class, you can adjust these numbers at your discretion, keeping in mind that bankers and stockbrokers should work in pairs and should not be responsible for too large an investor client base. Every investor is assigned to a specific banker-broker pair.

There are a total of four students serving as bankers, two each for Bank A and Bank B. Four students also play the role of stockbroker, two each in Brokerage Houses A and B. The remaining 12 students play investors and are assigned to the brokers and bankers as shown in the diagram. Each of these investors works with an assigned banker-broker pair.

MONTHLY MARKET REPORT

Disney Stock

Monthly average	Bonds (rate = 5%)	Equities opening	Equities closing
January		$34.50	$36.75
February		$36.75	$32.25
March		$32.25	$32.25
April		$32.25	$34.90
May		$34.90	$36.80
June		$36.50	$38.50
Total return			

Name:_____   Date: _____

ACTIVITY A

MEETING MR. PEEBLES

You are the financial director of the investment firm Morris, Oliver, Norton, Ester, and Young. A new client named Mr. Peebles is coming to you for expert financial advice. He will be arriving in your office in 10 minutes. Yesterday, in a telephone conversation with this client, you learned that he knows very little about investing and that he is a big Disney fan—he loves Disney movies, Disney TV, and Disney World. You decide to use the provided chart to explain how Disney stock has performed in the first half of the year. Answer the following questions in preparation for your meeting.

1. When you invest in a company and that investment is _____ (dependent on / independent of) the company's profits, the investments are called equities.

2. When you invest in a company and that investment is _____ (dependent on / independent of) the company's profits, the investments are called bonds.

3. _____ are risky investments, but taking more risk can lead to a _____.

4. If you purchased three shares of Disney stock on January 1st and sold them on June 30th, how much would you have earned/lost? _____
    Hint: (3 x closing price in June) – (3 x opening price in January) = return
    (3 x _____) – (3 x _____) = _____

5. If you bought $100 of Disney bonds on January 1st and sold them on June 30th, how much would you have earned/lost? _____
    Hint: purchase price x rate x term = return
    _____ x _____ x _____ = _____
    (Remember that the term is expressed in years, not months!)

ACTIVITY B

MEETING MR. PEEBLES

You are the financial director of the investment firm Morris, Oliver, Norton, Ester, and Young. A new client named Mr. Peebles is coming to you for expert financial advice. He will be arriving in your office in 10 minutes. Yesterday, in a telephone conversation with this client, you learned that he knows very little about investing and that he is a big Disney fan—he loves Disney movies, Disney TV, and Disney World. You decide to use the provided chart to explain how Disney stock has performed in the first half of the year. Answer the following questions in preparation for your meeting.

1. Write definitions for the following terms:

    Equities _____

    Bonds _____

    Return on investment _____

2. If you purchased three shares of Disney stock on January 1st and sold them on June 30th, how much would you have earned/lost?

3. If you bought $100 of Disney bonds on January 1st and sold them on June 30th, how much would you have earned/lost?

ACTIVITY C

MEETING MR. PEEBLES

You are the financial director of the investment firm Morris, Oliver, Norton, Ester, and Young. A new client named Mr. Peebles is coming to you for expert financial advice. He will be arriving in your office in 10 minutes. Yesterday, in a telephone conversation with this client, you learned that he knows very little about investing and that he is a big Disney fan—he loves Disney movies, Disney TV, and Disney World. You decide to use the provided chart to explain how Disney stock has performed in the first half of the year. Answer the following questions in preparation for your meeting.

1. Write definitions for the following terms:

    Equities _____

    Bonds _____

    Return on investment _____

2. Using the provided chart, show Mr. Peebles the difference he would have seen if he'd invested in Disney stock from January 1st to June 30th, as compared with investing in bonds for the same period.

ANSWER KEY

MEETING MR. PEEBLES

You are the financial director of the investment firm Morris, Oliver, Norton, Ester, and Young. A new client named Mr. Peebles is coming to you for expert financial advice. He will be arriving in your office in 10 minutes. Yesterday, in a telephone conversation with this client, you learned that he knows very little about investing and that he is a big Disney fan—he loves Disney movies, Disney TV, and Disney World. You decide to use the provided chart to explain how Disney stock has performed in the first half of the year. Answer the following questions in preparation for your meeting.

Activity A

1. When you invest in a company and that investment is **dependent on** the company's profits, the investments are called equities.
2. When you invest in a company and that investment is **independent of** the company's profits, the investments are called bonds.
3. **Stocks** are risky investments, but taking more risk can lead to a **greater return**.
4. If you purchased three shares of Disney stock on January 1st and sold them on June 30th, how much would you have earned/lost?
   Hint: (3 x closing price in June) – (3 x opening price in January) = return
   (3 x **$38.50**) – (3 x **$34.50**) = **$12**
5. If you bought $100 of Disney bonds on January 1st and sold them on June 30th, how much would you have earned/lost?
   Hint: purchase price x rate x term = return
   100 x .05 x .5 = $2.50

Activity B

Equities: risk interests of ownership (stock) in a corporation

Bonds: partial ownership of a corporation, secured by that corporation's physical assets

Return on investment (ROI): the percentage or amount of assets (money) earned as the result of making an investment; can be either positive or negative

If you purchased three shares of Disney stock on January 1st and sold them on June 30th, you would have earned $12. (See answers for Activity A for reasoning.)

If you bought $100 of Disney bonds on January 1st and sold them on June 30th, you would have earned $2.50. (See answers for Activity A for reasoning.)

Activity C

See answers for Activity B for definitions.

To determine the difference in returns, calculate the returns on investment and find the difference.
ROI (Disney stock) − ROI (Disney bonds)
(3 x 38.50 − 3 x 34.50) − (100 x .05 x .5)
$12 − $2.50
$9.50

Therefore, had Mr. Peebles chosen to invest in Disney stock, he would have realized a gain of $9.50 more than he would have had he invested in Disney bonds. This is the same as saying that he could have made $9.50 more investing in stock than he could have made investing in bonds.

Lesson 4

Concepts

- Understanding and using daily reports

Materials

- Investor prompt (p. 45)
- Example Investor Daily Report sheet (p. 46)
- Stockbroker prompt (p. 47)
- Example Stockbroker Daily Report sheet (p. 48)
- Banker prompt (p. 49)
- Banker tutorial (pp. 50–62)
- Example Banker Daily Report sheet (customer copy; pp. 57-58)
- Resource lesson (pp. 63)
- Activity A sheet (p. 64)
- Activity B sheet (p. 65)
- Activity C sheet (p. 66)
- Answer key (p. 67)
- Guide to Corporations sheet (p. 68)

Student Objective

The student learns to use daily report records and forms in this 2-day instructional lesson.

Introduction

Students are assigned the roles they will play for the remainder of the unit. Students are grouped by role and then learn to use the forms pertaining to their jobs.

Recognition

Students work with partners to demonstrate that they understand the various components of daily reports.

Application

Students work through examples and arrive at appropriate solutions on the daily report forms they have been assigned.

1. All brokers and investors should complete, with the assistance of the teacher, the following forms:
    *   Example Investor Daily Report sheet
    *   Example Stockbroker Daily Report sheet
    *   Example Banker Daily Report sheet (customer copy)

2. Bankers should work on the banker tutorial.
3. The provided resource lessons are for all students, particularly those who are experiencing difficulty with the math content.
4. If students who are playing stockbrokers and investors have extra time (which was rare in our experience), they may work on the banker tutorial to increase their knowledge of content operations.
5. We have provided additional resource lessons for any student to use, regardless of his or her role. These lessons may be especially useful for students having difficulty.

Problem Solving

Students develop their own original scenarios and perform the necessary calculations for completing their daily report forms to gain practice.

1. Have students create a character similar to Mr. Peebles, with interests, motivations, and other real-life attributes.
2. Students should research conditions surrounding an actual company (e.g., Apple) listed on a stock exchange.
3. They should use this information to carry out practice calculations that lead to a determination of the difference in returns.

Grade-Level Expectations

The student:

*   Communicates his or her understanding of mathematics and is able to use mathematical symbols and notation.
*   Formulates questions, conjectures, definitions, and generalizations about data, information, and problem situations.
*   Demonstrates conceptual understanding of mathematical operations by adding and subtracting positive fractions and integers and multiplying and dividing fractions and decimals.

- Accurately solves problems involving single or multiple operations on decimals, addition and subtraction of integers, and percentages of a whole.
- Uses a variety of mental computation strategies to solve problems and to determine the reasonableness of answers.

Additional Notes

- Use this lesson to teach students how to perform their assigned roles, stressing that every student must understand his or her role and how the roles interact (e.g., investors should understand what stockbrokers are doing with their money). We have provided sample versions of the forms that students will be using during the simulation. Reproducible blank forms are included in the next lesson; however, if you wish, you may continue to use the sample versions so that students can refer to the examples. As bankers are working on the banker tutorial, have investors and stockbrokers use the Investor Daily Report, the Banker Daily Report (customer copy), and the Stockbroker Daily Report sheets. Make sure that both investors and stockbrokers understand and work through all of these forms, stressing the importance of every student understanding all three roles and their interactions. Having students work through each form provides a mechanism with which to address content issues (e.g., decimals, percentages, fractions). The banker tutorial is formatted so that bankers will need very little teacher assistance, leaving you free to help investors and stockbrokers. The resource lesson can be used to supplement teaching, along with the provided activity sheets. Activity A is easiest, Activity B requires more advanced thinking, and Activity C is the most difficult.
- If you choose to give stockbrokers and bankers the option of investing, you might add on to the provided prompts to include this information. If you choose to do this, explain to stockbrokers that they may invest the money they earn off of their 5% commission rate. (They take 5% out of the money their clients invest; for instance, if a client wanted to invest $100, the broker would get $5, leaving the actual money available for investment at $95.) Bankers can invest portions of the money their banks are paid by the federal government at your discretion.
- We have provided a guide of the corporations discussed in this unit, although not all of them are investment options. (This is discussed further in the next lesson.)
- There are many forms to be kept track of in this unit. We have found that organization is essential, and what has worked best for us is to have each student keep all of his or her documents in a pocket folder. Then, all of the folders can be stored in one bin or central location—otherwise, students are likely to leave their materials at home.
- This lesson usually requires at least two (50-minute) periods to complete.

INVESTOR PROMPT

To our dearest grandchild,

For your birthday, your grandmother and I have given you $10,000 to invest in stocks. We went through some newspapers and used the Internet to narrow down your investment options. You will have the liberty to buy and sell as many shares in as many stocks as you like. Beginning tomorrow, the closing and opening stock prices will be listed daily. A newspaper will be posted with articles and information relating to the activities of some of the companies in which you may be investing. This information could be relevant to your decision-making process!

At the end of the week, we would like you to send us a letter explaining how you chose to invest your money, including how much you earned or lost. We will be interested to know why and how you made your decisions. Which stocks did you buy and sell along the way? How did you choose them? Where did you get your information? What investment lessons and strategies did you learn?

We wish that we could be there to watch you work firsthand—but unfortunately, our health prevents it. Please let us know exactly how you used the money. Include records of your transactions, graphs, tables or charts that show the results of your decisions, and anything else that will help us understand your strategies.

We are confident in your abilities. We look forward to reading your upcoming letter and seeing your visual aids!

With fondest wishes,

Grandpop & Grandma

Joseph M. Smith & Mary Louise Smith

These prompts were based on the work of Drs. Moon, Brighton, Callahan, and Tomlinson under the Educational and Research Centers PR/Award Number R206R50001. All rights permission secured.

Investor: _____   Date: _____

EXAMPLE INVESTOR DAILY REPORT

Transaction	Stock acquisition					Stock sales			
	A Amount of money withdrawn	B Broker's fee of 5% (.05 x A)	C Amount available to invest (A – B)	D Investment option / Purchase price	E Number of shares purchased (C ÷ D)	F1 Number of shares sold / F2 Sale price	G Return F1 x F2	H Proceeds G – (B + C)	I ROI (%) ((G – C) ÷ C) x 100
1	$4,000	$200	$3,800	Disney / $35	108.571	108.571 / $38	$4,125.70	$125.70	8.57%
2									
3									
4									
TOTALS									

Mathematics in the Marketplace © Prufrock Press Inc.

STOCKBROKER PROMPT

CoVelt Investments

Welcome aboard!

You have been hired as a stockbroker for the prestigious firm CoVelt. This is a wonderful opportunity for you! You have been hired to work with our clients and to advise them on how to invest their money. You must also keep track of all of their transactions in the stock market.

You will be assigned a group of first-time investors who have each been given $10,000 to invest as they see fit. Your responsibility is to counsel them to invest their wealth in profitable companies. The more they follow your good advice, the more money they will make. The more money they invest, the more money our firm makes! Also, you will be paid a 5% commission on all of your customers' investments. This means that if a customer decides to invest $100, then you make $5.

At the end of this unit, you will be asked to present your work to our Board of Directors. You must be able to document your customers' patterns of investment and how much money they earned. Please include what you advised your customers to do and how you decided to provide that advice. Document everything! A visual aid will be required to present your work effectively. The bottom line will be how much money you are able to make for our firm, CoVelt Investments!

Sincerely,

Richard Cote, Senior Partner

These prompts were based on the work of Drs. Moon, Brighton, Callahan, and Tomlinson under the Educational and Research Centers PR/Award Number R206R50001. All rights permission secured.

Stockbroker: _____ Date: _____

EXAMPLE STOCKBROKER DAILY REPORT

| Transaction | Stock acquisition | | | | Stock sales | | |
	A Initial capital	B Broker's fee of 5% (.05 x A)	C Amount available to invest (A – B)	D Investment option Purchase price	E Number of shares purchased (C ÷ D)	F1 Number of shares sold F2 Sale price	G Return F1 x F2	H Proceeds G – (B + C)
1	$4,000	$200	$3,800	Disney $35	108.571	108.571 $38	$4,125.70	$125.70
2								
3								
4								
TOTALS								

BANKER PROMPT

Congratulations!

You have been hired as Junior Vice President of The National Bank. You will be in charge of new customers' accounts. As you begin your work, remember that all of our customers' money, while available to them when they require it, can also be used as loan money for other customers. While the bank is "holding" its customers' money, that money earns 4% interest! Therefore, while money in the customers' accounts is earning them 2% daily, it is earning the bank 4% interest each day.

Your primary responsibility will be to track a set of new customers' accounts. The bank is interested in looking at the patterns of customers' withdrawals and deposits. Each of these customers has $10,000 on deposit with your bank to invest as he or she sees fit, and each bank has a beginning balance of an additional $50,000. These customers are all new investors. Do their withdrawals increase over time? Are they earning more in the stock market then they would if they left their money in our bank? The National Bank would like to see them invest their newfound wealth right here in our bank! Of course, you have to follow their wishes, but the more money they leave in their accounts overnight, the more money the bank will earn. You must find a balance between providing accurate accounting for your customers and counseling them to leave as much money as possible in the bank, where it is guaranteed to earn them 2% a day. What strategies would you recommend to entice customers to leave more of their money in the bank? How would this affect the bank's profits?

At the end of the week, we want you to present your work to the Board of Directors for their review. It is important that they be able to understand your rationale! Be sure to include visual aids to demonstrate how you tracked the customers' accounts and the money they earned, how your customers' strategies affected their final balances, and the amount of interest that was earned by the bank.

Good luck, and welcome aboard.

Frank O'Hara
Senior Vice President, The National Bank

These prompts were based on the work of Drs. Moon, Brighton, Callahan, and Tomlinson under the Educational and Research Centers PR/Award Number R206R50001. All rights permission secured.

BANKER TUTORIAL

Using this tutorial, you and your partner will prepare for the stock market to open while your classmates work on understanding the other roles (stockbroker and investor) that are needed for the unit to operate smoothly.

In general, the idea is for your bank to make money by satisfying investors' and stockbrokers' needs, as well as your own needs. The money business looks something like this:

You'll need to know some vocabulary first. It's important that you understand what *principal*, *rate*, *interest*, and *term* mean.

- **Principal:** the amount of money saved or borrowed
- **Rate:** the percentage the bank pays or charges its customers
- **Interest:** the amount of money the bank pays or charges its customers, or the amount of money the bank makes from the federal government
- **Term:** the length of time for which money is borrowed or loaned

There is a formula that brings all of these terms together so that you can do calculations.

$$I = P \times R \times T$$
I = interest
P = principal
R = rate
T = term

In real life, T—the term—measures time in years. In this unit, however, the term will be measured in days. In other words, a T value of 1 means 1 day, instead of 1 year.

Money will flow into your bank when investors and stockbrokers make deposits. To encourage citizens to deposit money into your bank, you will pay interest to your customers at the rate of 2% on any amount they leave in the bank overnight.

Name:_____ Date: _____

This means that although they are not making as much money as they could in a higher risk situation, such as stock investments, their money is secure and will definitely earn them a return.

Let's consider the formula I = P x R x T again to see how it can be used to satisfy your customers' need to make money.

EXAMPLE 1: Linda opens a savings account on a Tuesday by depositing $800 in your bank. To determine how much money she will have in the bank on Wednesday, let us use the formula I = P x R x T.

$$I = P \text{ x } R \text{ x } T$$
$$P = \$800$$
$$R = .02$$
$$T = 1$$
$$800 \text{ x } .02 \text{ x } 1 = 16$$

The amount of the deposit is called the principal, in this case $800. The percentage that your bank paid her is the rate, in this case 2%. The amount of time Linda's money is in the bank is called the term, in this case 1 day. The amount of money the bank pays to Linda is the interest, in this case $16.

By multiplying principal by rate by time, we get interest. Therefore, the next day (Wednesday), when Linda comes into the bank, she finds that she has $816 in her savings account. This is the original principal of $800 plus the interest, $16.

REMEMBER! In order to multiply by a percent, whatever percentage you are using must be represented in decimal form by moving the decimal point two places to the left. For example, 2% = .02.

EXAMPLE 2: Fred deposits $875 overnight. How much money does he have the next day?

$$I = P \text{ x } R \text{ x } T$$
$$P = \$875$$
$$R = 2\%$$
$$T = 1 \text{ day}$$
$$875 \text{ x } .02 \text{ x } 1 = 17.50$$

Using the formula, you can see that when Fred returns to your bank the next day, he finds that he has $892.50 in his account—the principal amount of $875 plus the interest of $17.50.

> **REMEMBER!** You may round off to the nearest cent if your calculations give you too many decimal places.

Try the following exercises individually, and then see whether your partner got the same answer that you did. Answers are provided below, but don't look ahead!

EXERCISE 1: A customer deposits $1,278 on Tuesday. What is the new balance on Wednesday?

EXERCISE 2: A customer deposits $1,400 on Monday. What is the new balance on Wednesday?

Check to see whether your answers are correct.
- **Exercise 1:** $1,303.56
- **Exercise 2:** $1,456.56 (Don't forget that because the term is two days, you must calculate the interest earned for the first night, and then use that total amount to calculate the interest earned for the second night.)

If you and your banking partner got these two problems correct, then you should move on. If your partner is confused, try to explain to him or her how to do the problem(s). If both you and your partner are confused, then try the practice problems in the Resource Lesson sheet and the sheets labeled Activity A, Activity B, and Activity C at the back of this packet. If your teacher has time, you might ask for additional help.

It will be necessary for you to keep track of your customers' savings accounts. You must also ensure that your customers know how to fill out copies to keep for their own records, because they will not have completed this tutorial.

Banking Forms

In this packet, there are two forms called Example Banker Daily Report. Pull these out and look at them frequently as you are reading. You will notice that one of these is to be kept by the banker (the banker copy), and one is to be kept by the customer (the customer copy).

Name:_____ Date: _____

You must ensure that the banker copy stays with the bank at all times. Also, these two copies must match up exactly. Always remember to put the date on these forms so that you can have a record of what happened on a given day.

You must be able to complete this form for your bank, and you must also be able to teach your customers how to maintain these forms for their own portfolios. Here is a description of each part of the daily report:

Column A (BALANCE): This is the amount of money customers have in the bank at the beginning of each day. It **must match up** with Column E from the prior day, which shows the customer's final balance (amount of money) from the day before. In other words, the amount of money that a customer has in the bank at the end of business on Tuesday must be equal to the amount that he or she has at the beginning of the day on Wednesday.

Column B (DEPOSITS): This is where you will enter any deposits that customers bring to your bank.

Column C (WITHDRAWALS): If a client takes money out of the bank (for example, if he or she needs money to buy stock), then this column is where you would write down the amount of money that he or she took out.

Column D (INTEREST): This is the column you will use to determine how much money a customer has in the bank at the end of the day and overnight (the final balance). You will need this number to figure out how much interest the customer is paid according to the amount that he or she has in the account.

Let's work through the example shown on the Example Banker Daily Report sheets. Look at the banker copy on p. 57.

Linda begins with a balance of $0 (this is shown in Column A). Linda deposits $2,000 into her savings account (this is shown in Column B). Because she runs out of time, she does not withdraw any of her money. Therefore, there is a "0" entered in Column C, so Linda is going to leave $2,000 in your bank overnight. She will earn interest on this amount, which you must calculate and enter in Column D.

> To calculate the amount of interest to enter in
> Column D, use the formula I = P x R x T.
>
> Because T is 1, we will not show it. The principal amount is
> the initial amount (Column A) plus the money that came
> into the account or left the account that day, meaning any
> deposits that were made (Column B) minus any withdrawals
> that were made (Column C). The new formula becomes
> .02 (A + (B − C)) = D, the interest paid on the account.
>
> Formula: .02 (A + (B − C)) = D
> Substitute: .02 (0 + ($2,000 − 0)) = D
> Solve: D = 40

So Linda earned $40 of interest on her account. This means that Linda's final balance is $2,040—if you look, you'll see that the banker copy and the customer copy both show this. It is very important that these forms match up exactly!

Try the following exercise on your own, and then check the sheet labeled Practice Banker Daily Report (p. 59) to see if you and your partner are on track.

EXERCISE 3: Linda comes to your bank on Day 2. She deposits an additional $11,500 and also withdraws $2,000 to meet some of her expenses. Calculate what her balance will be at the beginning of Day 3.

Check the practice sheet to see whether you are correct. If you and your partner are both confused, speak with your teacher. If not, then it is time to learn how *you* get to make money!

Bank Earnings

You are paying customers 2% on the amounts they have deposited in your bank overnight. However, the federal government (represented by your teacher) pays your bank 4% on the amount of money in your bank overnight.

In addition, your bank will be opening with an initial deposit of $50,000 in addition to the money deposited by investors. The way interest is calculated for your bank is the same way that interest is calculated for your customers. The difference is that you get 4%, whereas your customers get 2%.

The Bank Daily Summary form must be filled out at the end of each day. It is a record showing how much money your bank will make by keeping money overnight.

Let's go through the example shown on the sheet labeled Example Bank Daily Summary.

This example shows a beginning balance of $50,000 (Column A). A total of six customers came to your bank to deposit a total of $13,500 (Column B) and made total withdrawals of $2,000 (Column C). Note carefully that the amount in Column B ($13,500) was calculated by adding up all of the deposits made by your customers. To do this, you will add all of the amounts in Column B of the Banker Daily Report sheets. The amount in Column C ($2,000) was calculated by finding the total amount withdrawn by all of your customers.

To calculate the amount of interest your bank will earn overnight from the federal government, use the formula shown in Column D of the Bank Daily Summary.

Formula: $(A + (B − C)) \times .04 = D$
Substitute: $(\$50,000 + (\$13,500 − \$2,000)) \times .04 = D$
Solve: $(\$50,000 + \$11,500) \times .04 = D$
$(\$61,500) \times .04 = D$
$\$2,460 = D$

So in this example, the federal government pays you $2,460 to have your money in this account overnight. Column E shows the amount you paid in interest to all of your customers. Remember that in Exercise 3, you paid Linda $230.80 in interest. Column E shows that amount added to all of the other interest amounts you had to pay to customers (this column shows the total amount of money the bank paid customers in interest). To calculate the bank's final balance at the end of the day, you will use the formula shown in Column F.

$A + B + D − C − E = F$
$\$50,000 + \$13,500 − \$2,000 + \$2,460 − \$230.80 = F$
$\$63,729.20 = F$

Notice that the balance in Column A on any given day should be the same as the final balance from the day before.

Try the following exercise, and then see if you are correct by checking the sheet labeled Practice Bank Daily Summary on p. 62.

EXERCISE 4: Let us say that on Day 2, four customers came to your bank to deposit a total of $6,500. Additionally, two other customers withdrew a total of $800.

Let us say that you paid out a total of $585 in interest to your customers. Determine your starting balance for Day 3.

Make sure that you are correct! Now you have learned about one way that the bank can make money: by taking in as much money as possible from investors and stockbrokers and keeping it overnight so that you earn 4% interest on their accounts.

Whew! We hope you have learned your lessons well—your clients are depending on you.

Banker: _____

Customer: _____ Date: _____

EXAMPLE BANKER DAILY REPORT
(Banker Copy)

Day	A Balance	B Deposits	C Withdrawals	D Interest (2%) $.02 \times (A + (B - C))=$	E Final balance $A + B + D - C$
1	0	$2,000	0	$2,000 \times .02 = $40	$2,040
2	$2,040				
3					
4					
Totals					

Customer: _____

Banker: _____ Date: _____

EXAMPLE BANKER DAILY REPORT
(Customer Copy)

Day	A Balance	B Deposits	C Withdrawals	D Interest (2%) .02 x (A + (B – C))=	E Final balance A + B + D – C
1	0	$2,000	0	$2,000 x .02 = $40	$2,040
2	$2,040				
3					
4					
Totals					

Banker: _____

Customer: _____   Date: _____

PRACTICE BANKER DAILY REPORT
(Banker Copy)

Day	A Balance	B Deposits	C Withdrawals	D Interest (2%) $.02 \times (A + (B - C)) =$	E Final balance $A + B + D - C$
1	0	$2,000	0	$2,000 x .02 = $40	$2,040
2	$2,040	$11,500	$2,000	(.02)($11,540) = $230.80	$11,770.80
3	$11,770.80				
4					
Totals					

Customer: _____

Banker: _____ Date: _____

PRACTICE BANKER DAILY REPORT
(Customer Copy)

Day	A Balance	B Deposits	C Withdrawals	D Interest (2%) $.02 \times (A + (B - C)) =$	E Final balance $A + B + D - C$
1	0	$2,000	0	$2,000 x .02 = $40	$2,040
2	$2,040	$11,500	$2,000	$(.02)($11,540)$ $= 230.80	$11,770.80
3	$11,770.80				
4					
Totals					

Banker:_____ Date:_____

EXAMPLE BANK DAILY SUMMARY

Transaction	A Balance	B Total deposits (from Banker Daily Reports)	C Total withdrawals (from Banker Daily Reports)	D Bank earnings (4%) $(A + (B - C))$ $\times .04 =$	E Total interest expenses (from Banker Daily Reports Column D)	F Final balance $A + B + D - C - E =$
1	$50,000	$13,500 (total from six customers)	$2,000	$2,460	$230	$63,729.20
2	$63,729.20					
3						
4						
Totals						

Banker: _____   Date: _____

PRACTICE BANK DAILY SUMMARY

Transaction	A Balance	B Total deposits (from Banker Daily Reports)	C Total withdrawals (from Banker Daily Reports)	D Bank earnings (4%) $(A + (B - C)) \times .04 =$	E Total interest expenses (from Banker Daily Reports Column D)	F Final balance $A + B + D - C - E =$
1	$50,000	$13,500 (total from six customers)	$2,000	$2,460	$230.80	$63,729.20
2	$63,729.20	$6,500	$800	$2,777.17	$585	$71,621.37
3	$71,621.37					
4						
Totals						

RESOURCE LESSON

The following lesson will help you understand decision variables and how to solve percent problems. You'll need to watch out for the word "of"!

When the word "of" <u>connects</u> two numbers, you will want to <u>multiply</u>.

Multiplication is commutative, which means that you can multiply the same set of numbers in any order and still get the same result. Therefore, it doesn't matter which number is the *multiplicand* (number to be multiplied) or which is the *multiplier* (number of times it is multiplied). Reminder: multiplicand x multiplier = product.

$$a \times b = b \times a$$

Example: _____ is 75% of 60. (Remember that to use percentages in equations, you should convert them to decimals. 75% is represented as .75.)
.75 x 60 = 45

When the word "of" <u>does not connect</u> two numbers, you will want to <u>divide</u>.

Division is not commutative. Order matters when you are dividing! The dividend (the numerator of the fraction, or what is being divided) and the divisor (the denominator of the fraction, or the number of times the dividend is being divided) must be in the correct places.

$$a \div b \neq b \div a$$

The first hint that may help you is that when the word "of" does not connect two numbers, and when the percentage is available, you should divide by the percentage.

Example: 8% of _____ is 22.
22 ÷ .08 = 275

If you cannot use the first helpful hint, then another helpful hint is that you should divide the smaller number by the larger number to find out what percentage of the larger number the smaller number makes up. Remember to move your decimal two places!

Example: What percent of 5.6 is .72?
.72 ÷ 5.6 = .1286 = 12.86%

ACTIVITY A

Do your work on a separate piece of paper, and make sure your name is on it. Attach your work to this sheet.

1. 113% of 650 is _____.

2. 76 is _____ percent of 200.

3. 80% of _____ is 250.

4. 48% of 64 is _____.

5. 250 is 80% of _____.

6. 15 is _____ percent of 60.

7. 46 is 84% of _____.

8. 12.5% of 63 is _____.

9. 46.7 is _____ percent of 90.

10. 326% of 68 is _____.

ACTIVITY B

Do your work on a separate piece of paper, and make sure your name is on it. Attach your work to this sheet.

1. In 1991, about 40% of the 52,000,000 married couples in America had two incomes. About how many couples had two incomes?
2. Twenty years ago, 210,000 women made up 11.5% of all military personnel. How many military personnel were there 20 years ago?
3. Sales tax on a video game is $3.08 in a state where the sales tax rate is 7%. What is the cost of the video game?

ACTIVITY C
. . . .

Do your work on a separate piece of paper, and make sure your name is on it. Attach your work to this sheet.

1. I went to my stockbroker with $3,800 to invest in Fuelstone's stock and told him I needed to have $100 left to buy my girlfriend a gift. If he charges me $48 for the transaction, then what is his rate of commission?

2. I deposited my paycheck in a new bank account that pays 2% per day on overnight deposits. The next day, I had $1,000 in my account. To the nearest cent, what was the value of my paycheck when I deposited it?

3. An investor bought 240 shares of Mega Systems stock at $19.85 per share. The stock was sold 6 weeks later for $6,000. The stockbroker charges a commission of 5% to purchase stock, and sales are free. Find the ROI as a percent. In this case, include the commission as part of your investment.

$$\text{ROI} = \left(\frac{\text{Return} - \text{Investment}}{\text{Investment}} \right) \times 100$$

ANSWER KEY

Activity A

1. 734.5
2. 38%
3. 312.5
4. 30.72
5. 312.5
6. 25%
7. Approximately 54.76
8. 7.875
9. Approximately 51.8%
10. 221.68

Activity B

1. 20,800,000
2. Approximately 1,826,087
3. $44

Activity C

1. Approximately 1.297%
2. $980.39 (paycheck + .02% paycheck = $1000)
3. $$\text{ROI} = \left(\frac{6,000 - 5,002.20}{5,002.20} \right) \times 100$$

   $$= \text{Approximately } 19.9\%$$

GUIDE TO CORPORATIONS

Bull's Eye (BUL): Midline retail discount chain

Cheese, Inc. (CHE): Dairy products distributor

Chocolog (CHL): Candy and dessert foods distributor

Chug (CHG): Large soft drink distributor

Clips (CLP): Retail office supplies chain

Corporal Bill (COB): Breakfast cereal distributor

cPhone (C): Cell phone manufacturer

Dash Telecom (DST): Cell phone provider network

FeeTab (FET): Credit card facilitator

Fuelstone's (FSTN): Midline retail discount chain

Gofigure (FIG): Upscale clothing store chain

Granny Smith (GRS): Extremely successful computer software company

Gulp (GUP): Large soft drink distributor

King Cola (KCO): World's largest soft drink company

Kringle's (KRK): Midscale retail store chain

Mega Systems (MST): Computer hardware and software corporation

Mooncent (MON): Specialty restaurant corporation

Packit (PKT): Computer hardware company

Pasture (PT): Computer hardware manufacturer

Perry Auto (PRTO): Automobile manufacturer

Quizet (QZT): Upscale retail chain

Sammy's (SAM): Large retail discount store chain

SchoolDays (SHD): School supplies distributor

Seven Stars (SES): Leisure park enterprise

Slurp Soups (SRP): Soup distribution company

Sneakerz (SNK): Specialty footwear manufacturer

Speed Demon (SPD): Worldwide package delivery service

Walt World (WTW): Leisure park giant

Lesson 5

Concepts

- Calculating gains and losses
- Investing in the stock market
- Savings accounts

Materials

- Investor Daily Report sheet (p. 72)
- Stockbroker Daily Report sheet (p. 73)
- Banker Daily Report sheet (banker copy; p. 74)
- Banker Daily Report sheet (customer copy; p. 75)
- Bank Daily Summary sheet (p. 76)
- *The Wall Street Gazette* (issues 1, 2, 3, and 4; pp. 77–80)
- Stock market tables (for days 1, 2, 3, 4, and 5; pp. 81–85)
- Stock certificates (p. 86)

Student Objective

The student demonstrates the ability to use percentages and decimals to manage his or her banker, stockbroker, or investor portfolio.

Introduction

Begin each day by posting or photocopying the appropriate issue of *The Wall Street Gazette*. Then post or photocopy the appropriate stock market table for the day. Give a hard copy of the stock market table to each stockbroker.

Recognition

Students should use the first 10 minutes of the class to check account balances, calculate gains and losses, and make decisions about what to buy and sell. Banks are open during this time to allow investors to withdraw money to buy stocks.

Application

For 25 minutes, students run a simulation of the stock market investment cycle.

1. The teacher rings a bell to signify that the market is open, and trading begins.
2. Investors withdraw the amounts of money they have decided to invest for the day.
3. Each banker initials the paperwork to verify to the stockbroker that the investor's money is available for investment.
4. Investors proceed to their brokers, and together they decide which stocks and how many shares of each stock will be bought. The broker and investor complete the paperwork for the transaction, including the stock certificate that is proof of ownership for the investor.
5. Investors deposit any excess funds into their savings accounts.
6. After 25 minutes of trading, the bell is rung and the market closes.

Problem Solving

Students spend the final 10 minutes of the class reconciling their accounts and completing the mathematical paperwork.

Grade-Level Expectations

The student:
- Analyzes patterns, trends, or distributions in data in a variety of contexts by determining or using measures of central tendency or dispersion to analyze situations or to solve problems.
- Demonstrates conceptual understanding of mathematical operations by adding and subtracting positive fractions and integers and by multiplying and dividing fractions and decimals.
- Accurately solves problems involving single or multiple operations on decimals, addition or subtraction of integers, and percentages of a whole.
- Uses a variety of mental computation strategies to solve problems and to determine the reasonableness of answers.
- Demonstrates conceptual understanding of algebraic expressions by using letters to represent unknown quantities to write linear algebraic expressions that involve any of the four operations and are consistent with orders of operations.
- Evaluates linear algebraic expressions or expressions within equations.

Additional Notes

- This lesson is really where the rubber meets the road, so to speak, and students actually get the chance to implement the concepts they have been using. You should expect students to experience some level of frustration as they realize that learning about roles does not necessarily mean that they will be able to perform perfectly or even successfully.
- In our experience, it will be immediately evident which students understand the content, as well as which ones are struggling. Do not be overwhelmed at the number of questions you will need to field—this is an ideal situation, wherein students need your instruction in order to complete practical tasks that interest them. Ideally, students will be able to help one another, also.
- If it seems that students are really shaky regarding content, you might deem it necessary to take a day off to review. Conversely, do not be afraid to let students work through their own problems. If you see that students are figuring out the concepts and assisting one another, wait before lending your help.
- The purpose of this unit is to provide a context that engages students, enabling them to demonstrate learning and occasionally encounter frustrations that spur them forward. Thus, there is no set formula for success; the information provided in *The Wall Street Gazette* and the stock tables is not comprehensive, nor does it have any one correct interpretation. In keeping with the volatility of the real-world stock market, many of the companies mentioned in *The Wall Street Gazette* are not even investment options, and while the issues do contain some hints (office supplies stock rises after a favorable article, for instance), there are also some red herrings. The point is for students to find their own paths in the unit. They must be able to defend their choices with logic and proof.

Investor: _____ Date: _____

INVESTOR DAILY REPORT

Transaction	A Amount of money withdrawn	B Broker's fee of 5% (.05 x A)	C Amount available to invest (A – B)	D Investment option Purchase price	E Number of shares purchased (C ÷ D)	F1 Number of shares sold / F2 Sale price	G Return F1 x F2	H Proceeds G – (B + C)	I ROI (%) ((G – C) ÷ C) x 100
	Stock acquisition					Stock sales			
1									
2									
3									
4									
TOTALS									

Stockbroker: _____ Date: _____

STOCKBROKER DAILY REPORT

Transaction	A Initial capital	B Broker's fee of 5% (.05 x A)	C Amount available to invest (A − B)	D Investment option Purchase price	E Number of shares purchased (C ÷ D)	F1 Number of shares sold F2 Sale price	G Return F1 x F2	H Proceeds G − (B + C)
			Stock acquisition			Stock sales		
1								
2								
3								
4								
TOTALS								

Banker: _____

Customer: _____ Date: _____

BANKER DAILY REPORT (Banker Copy)

Day	A Balance	B Deposits	C Withdrawals	D Interest (2%) $.02 \times (A + (B - C)) =$	E Final balance $A + B + D - C$
1					
2					
3					
4					
Totals					

Mathematics in the Marketplace © Prufrock Press Inc.

Customer: _____

Banker: _____ Date: _____

BANKER DAILY REPORT (Customer Copy)

Day	A Balance	B Deposits	C Withdrawals	D Interest (2%) .02 x (A + (B − C))=	E Final balance A + B + D − C
1					
2					
3					
4					
Totals					

Banker: _____   Date: _____

BANK DAILY SUMMARY

Transaction	A Balance	B Total deposits (from Banker Daily Reports)	C Total withdrawals (from Banker Daily Reports)	D Bank earnings (4%) $(A + (B - C))$ $\times .04 =$	E Total interest expenses (from Banker Daily Reports Column D)	F Final balance $A + B + D - C - E =$
1						
2						
3						
4						
Totals						

Mathematics in the Marketplace © Prufrock Press Inc.

PACKIT RELEASES A NEW LINE OF LAPTOPS

Packit is winning the computer wars this week

The computer giant Packit has announced the release of a new, groundbreaking line of laptop computers. These machines are guaranteed a large share of the computer market with their guaranteed ability to block any and all viruses. In addition to their superior security features, they have high-definition screens and can pick up a wireless signal anywhere in the world! Their software allows them to talk to any other computer effortlessly. This capability makes them the most versatile computers to date.

Competitor computer company Mega Systems vows to outperform this technology with its next addition to an already overcrowded market. However, Packit has certainly outpaced Mega Systems in getting these new laptops to the market first. Prerelease sales have already netted Packit more than $6 million dollars, which guarantees that its stock values will rise sharply.

BULL'S EYE OPENS STORE NUMBER 5,000

Bull's Eye announced today that it is set to open its 5,000th store on Saturday. The giant department store has changed the way America shops. By increasing its buying power with so many stores, Bull's Eye is able to offer lower prices to its customers. Unlike its chief rival, Sammy's, Bull's Eye has a good reputation for taking care of its employees and giving back to the community. This has helped the Bull's Eye Corporation to increase its profits yearly since it first opened its doors in 1990. Don't miss the opening day festivities, with free ice cream and soda and lots of entertainment for the kids!

Curl up with a hearty bowl of Slurp Soup

BULL'S EYE
You need it, we've got it.

Weather update:

More snow is predicted in our area today. A storm will move through the region beginning in the early morning hours and continuing throughout the day. This storm system is expected to dump more than 48 inches, a local record.

NATURE VS. FEETAB: NATURE 1, FEETAB 0!

Disaster strikes at the heart of North American operations

The North American headquarters for credit card company FeeTab, located in the heart of New York City, was struck by lightning yesterday. The massive electrical strike overwhelmed the protective mechanisms usually in place and shut down all of the computers in the building. This shutdown has affected stores across the country, forcing them to use ancient methods of recordkeeping, such as hand running and checking all the FeeTab cards presented at their cashiers' stations. Salespeople from Sacramento, CA, to Portland, ME are tearing their hair out trying to meet their customers' needs.

The situation begs the question of how America would survive if all power were lost for a considerable length of time. Have we, as a nation, become so dependent on technology that we can no longer survive without it? In an interview with Mr. Ezra Carroll, C.E.O. of FeeTab, he assured us, "The systems will be back up and running by nightfall!" He also wanted to make clear that this disaster did not put any customers' private account information at risk. The lesson here seems to be that when Mother Nature does her worst, Americans have no choice but to be patient!

STORES REPORT INCREASED EARNINGS RESULTING FROM HOME OFFICES

More and more people are deciding to work from home, where they have control over their own hours, office setups, and thermostats—and they're not the only ones reaping the benefits. In a suffering economy, office suppliers are reporting increased sales.

"We were bracing ourselves for some bad figures, but we were pleasantly surprised to find that even people who are out of work are buying more office supplies than usual," said Rufus Chifari, President of Clips, an office supplier. Chifari, who is notoriously eccentric, decorated his own home office with framed turkey recipes and clocks made out of limited-edition board games. "That's the beauty of home offices," he said enthusiastically. "You can personalize them however you want."

These days, everybody has a home office: bosses squeezing in extra hours, parents who want to stay home with their children, freelance workers, and even those without jobs who need organized environments where they can search for employment and prepare for interviews. Technology such as videoconferencing has made home offices practical and easy, and office supply stores have equipment that buyers can use to satisfy all of their needs—ranging from the everyday to the unusual. "For my next home office project, I'm building an elaborate system of pulleys using magnets and wire mesh pencil holders," noted Chifari.

Weather update:

Terrible thunderstorms are predicted to hit the nearby metropolitan area late this afternoon, moving steadily west. The rain is expected to dissipate by midnight at the latest.

JIMMY GOFIGURE AND QUIZET TEAM UP TO BENEFIT THE POOR

Fashion giants Jimmy Gofigure and Quizet have agreed to partner for a charity benefit concert and fashion show to help fight world hunger. This crowd-pleasing event will be held during the height of fashion week in New York City and is expected to raise millions for the soup kitchens of the city's poverty-stricken population. James McMiller, a spokesperson for Gofigure, said, "We are all concerned that the people of the world are starving while we, who are successful, have way more than we need. This is Jimmy's way of giving back."

The fashion giants have come together to fight world hunger.

Several popular musicians have already committed to the effort, as well as dozens of high-profile fashion models. Tickets will be available through both Gofigure and Quizet stores and are scheduled to go on sale next week. Sandra Landback, a spokesperson for Quizet, said, "This is a wonderful opportunity for us to show people that the world of fashion is not some sort of egocentric organism that only feeds consumerism. This is a chance for us to feed people in need."

SUGAR CROPS DAMAGED BY MYSTERIOUS DROUGHT IN PUERTO RICO

Puerto Rican authorities have reported that a mysterious drought is damaging the sugar crop of America's small island territory. In a normal year, the United States—including Puerto Rico—would produce around 6.87 million metric tons of raw sugar. This year, there is great concern that this number will fall drastically due to a severe and little-understood drought. In a region that generally gets about 171 inches of rain a year, this year, the island will have seen fewer than only 75 inches.

This reduction in rainfall greatly impacts the volume of sugar cane that can be grown. American industries are quite concerned about how this will impact the cost of sugar imports, and the resulting price raises they will be forced to impose on products.

Weather update:

Warmer than usual temperatures and bountiful sunshine is expected today, although temperatures will drop this evening and yield to colder, rainier weather tomorrow and throughout the weekend.

THE WALL STREET GAZETTE

SPEED DEMON SHIPPING CELEBRATES EXCELLENT DRIVERS' RECORDS

Delivery company Speed Demon has announced that it will reward company drivers who have maintained accident-free records for 10 years or more. The company was proud to include more than 300 of its drivers, hailing from all over the world. These drivers will be given monetary awards and plaques during a special event slated to be held at the delivery giant's headquarters. Speed Demon maintains that its drivers are the safest in the world, allowing the company to better serve its customers' needs around the globe.

In a related story, three drivers representing Speed Demon, Inc., operating companies were crowned national champions at this year's annual National Truck Driving Championships (NTDC) in Houston last month. "Collectively, SpeDe drivers and contractors around the world are focused on safely sharing the roads with other motorists each and every day," said Wayne F. Smith, chairman, president, and C.E.O. of Speed Demon. "The performances of the 70 drivers who earned the right to compete at the NTDC, and the performances of the top finishers in particular, reaffirms this company's fundamental commitment to safety and professionalism."

DIET GULP OFFICIALLY AMERICA'S FAVORITE SODA

In a nationwide survey released today, Diet Gulp is revealed to be America's favorite soda by an overwhelming majority. The Gulp Company was thrilled with the survey's findings.

A spokesperson for competitor soda giant Chug, however, called into question the legitimacy of the survey's results, maintaining that Chug has conducted surveys that show very different results. "The Chug Cola company is appalled that Gulp would be so na-ive as to think that anyone would be convinced by such a shallow attempt at false advertising!" said Jenna Smits, Chug spokesperson.

The National Survey Institute, the company responsible for the survey, refutes Chug's claim that their survey could be fallible. The NSI claims that its test group was very large, its results were significant, and Chug simply has a bad case of "sour grapes," according to one NSI employee who wished to remain unnamed.

Chocolog, Inc. publicly apologizes for the mistaken addition of soap to a batch of Choco-Loco bubble gum last month. All packages dated prior to one week ago should be discarded or returned to the store for an immediate cash refund.

The Gulp vs. Chug challenge

Which do *you* drink?

Weather update:

The rain expected for today will hold off until tomorrow, giving the area an extra day of sunshine before a cold front blows in.

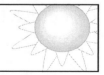

STOCK MARKET TABLE 1

Ticker	Company	Opening 1
BUL	Bull's Eye	$68.25
CHE	Cheese, Inc.	$48.50
CHG	Chug	$66.50
CHL	Chocolog	$28.50
CLP	Clips	$24.75
COB	Corporal Bill	$59.00
DST	Dash Telecom	$21.75
FET	FeeTab	$167.50
FSTN	Fuelstone's	$71.50
KCO	King Cola	$53.00
KRK	Kringle's	$43.00
MON	Mooncent	$26.75
PRTO	Perry Auto	$41.00
PT	Pasture	$29.00
QZT	Quizet	$52.00
SES	Seven Stars	$6.00
SHD	SchoolDays	$36.50
SNK	Sneakerz	$60.00
SPD	Speed Demon	$111.75
SRP	Slurp Soups	$39.25
WTW	Walt World	$34.50

STOCK MARKET TABLE 2

Ticker	Company	Opening 1	Closing 1	Opening 2
BUL	Bull's Eye	$68.25	$71.00	$71.00
CHE	Cheese, Inc.	$48.50	$53.00	$53.00
CHG	Chug	$66.50	$72.75	$72.75
CHL	Chocolog	$28.50	$25.00	$25.00
CLP	Clips	$24.75	$27.00	$27.00
COB	Corporal Bill	$59.00	$52.00	$52.00
DST	Dash Telecom	$21.75	$30.00	$30.00
FET	FeeTab	$167.50	$170.00	$170.00
FSTN	Fuelstone's	$71.50	$74.00	$74.00
KCO	King Cola	$53.00	$60.00	$60.00
KRK	Kringle's	$43.00	$40.00	$40.00
MON	Mooncent	$26.75	$25.00	$25.00
PRTO	Perry Auto	$41.00	$36.00	$36.00
PT	Pasture	$29.00	$25.00	$25.00
QZT	Quizet	$52.00	$53.50	$53.50
SES	Seven Stars	$6.00	$6.25	$6.25
SHD	SchoolDays	$36.50	$39.50	$39.50
SNK	Sneakerz	$60.00	$55.00	$55.00
SPD	Speed Demon	$111.75	$120.00	$120.00
SRP	Slurp Soups	$39.25	$36.00	$36.00
WTW	Walt World	$34.50	$34.50	$34.50

STOCK MARKET TABLE 3

Ticker	Company	Opening 1	Closing 1	Opening 2	Closing 2	Opening 3
BUL	Bull's Eye	$68.25	$71.00	$71.00	$72.50	$72.50
CHE	Cheese, Inc.	$48.50	$53.00	$53.00	$54.00	$54.00
CHG	Chug	$66.50	$72.75	$72.75	$75.00	$75.00
CHL	Chocolog	$28.50	$25.00	$25.00	$24.00	$24.00
CLP	Clips	$24.75	$27.00	$27.00	$30.00	$30.00
COB	Corporal Bill	$59.00	$52.00	$52.00	$50.00	$50.00
DST	Dash Telecom	$21.75	$30.00	$30.00	$33.00	$33.00
FET	FeeTab	$167.50	$170.00	$170.00	$160.00	$160.00
FSTN	Fuelstone's	$71.50	$74.00	$74.00	$77.00	$77.00
KCO	King Cola	$53.00	$60.00	$60.00	$62.50	$62.50
KRK	Kringle's	$43.00	$40.00	$40.00	$37.00	$37.00
MON	Mooncent	$26.75	$25.00	$25.00	$23.00	$23.00
PRTO	Perry Auto	$41.00	$36.00	$36.00	$37.50	$37.50
PT	Pasture	$29.00	$25.00	$25.00	$24.00	$24.00
QZT	Quizet	$52.00	$53.50	$53.50	$56.00	$56.00
SES	Seven Stars	$6.00	$6.25	$6.25	$6.00	$6.00
SHD	SchoolDays	$36.50	$39.50	$39.50	$44.00	$44.00
SNK	Sneakerz	$60.00	$55.00	$55.00	$56.50	$56.50
SPD	Speed Demon	$111.75	$120.00	$120.00	$122.00	$122.00
SRP	Slurp Soups	$39.25	$36.00	$36.00	$35.50	$35.50
WTW	Walt World	$34.50	$34.50	$34.50	$36.75	$36.75

STOCK MARKET TABLE 4

Ticker	Company	Opening 1	Closing 1	Opening 2	Closing 2	Opening 3	Closing 3	Opening 4
BUL	Bull's Eye	$68.25	$71.00	$71.00	$72.50	$72.50	$74.00	$74.00
CHE	Cheese, Inc.	$48.50	$53.00	$53.00	$54.00	$54.00	$55.00	$55.00
CHG	Chug	$66.50	$72.75	$72.75	$75.00	$75.00	$78.00	$78.00
CHL	Chocolog	$28.50	$25.00	$25.00	$24.00	$24.00	$21.00	$21.00
CLP	Clips	$24.75	$27.00	$27.00	$30.00	$30.00	$32.50	$32.50
COB	Corporal Bill	$59.00	$52.00	$52.00	$50.00	$50.00	$48.00	$48.00
DST	Dash Telecom	$21.75	$30.00	$30.00	$33.00	$33.00	$30.00	$30.00
FET	FeeTab	$167.50	$170.00	$170.00	$160.00	$160.00	$164.00	$164.00
FSTN	Fuelstone's	$71.50	$74.00	$74.00	$77.00	$77.00	$74.00	$74.00
KCO	King Cola	$53.00	$60.00	$60.00	$62.50	$62.50	$61.00	$61.00
KRK	Kringle's	$43.00	$40.00	$40.00	$37.00	$37.00	$35.50	$35.50
MON	Mooncent	$26.75	$25.00	$25.00	$23.00	$23.00	$20.75	$20.75
PRTO	Perry Auto	$41.00	$36.00	$36.00	$37.50	$37.50	$40.00	$40.00
PT	Pasture	$29.00	$25.00	$25.00	$24.00	$24.00	$26.00	$26.00
QZT	Quizet	$52.00	$53.50	$53.50	$56.00	$56.00	$59.00	$59.00
SES	Seven Stars	$6.00	$6.25	$6.25	$6.00	$6.00	$7.00	$7.00
SHD	SchoolDays	$36.50	$39.50	$39.50	$44.00	$44.00	$46.00	$46.00
SNK	Sneakerz	$60.00	$55.00	$55.00	$56.50	$56.50	$54.50	$54.50
SPD	Speed Demon	$111.75	$120.00	$120.00	$122.00	$122.00	$125.00	$125.00
SRP	Slurp Soups	$39.25	$36.00	$36.00	$35.50	$35.50	$36.50	$36.50
WTW	Walt World	$34.50	$34.50	$34.50	$36.75	$36.75	$37.25	$37.25

STOCK MARKET TABLE 5

Ticker	Company	Opening 1	Closing 1	Opening 2	Closing 2	Opening 3	Closing 3	Opening 4	Closing 4
BUL	Bull's Eye	$68.25	$71.00	$71.00	$72.50	$72.50	$74.00	$74.00	$75.50
CHE	Cheese, Inc.	$48.50	$53.00	$53.00	$54.00	$54.00	$55.00	$55.00	$55.60
CHG	Chug	$66.50	$72.75	$72.75	$75.00	$75.00	$78.00	$78.00	$78.75
CHL	Chocolog	$28.50	$25.00	$25.00	$24.00	$24.00	$21.00	$21.00	$20.60
CLP	Clips	$24.75	$27.00	$27.00	$30.00	$30.00	$32.50	$32.50	$34.00
COB	Corporal Bill	$59.00	$52.00	$52.00	$50.00	$50.00	$48.00	$48.00	$47.00
DST	Dash Telecom	$21.75	$30.00	$30.00	$33.00	$33.00	$30.00	$30.00	$28.00
FET	FeeTab	$167.50	$170.00	$170.00	$160.00	$160.00	$164.00	$164.00	$172.00
FSTN	Fuelstone's	$71.50	$74.00	$74.00	$77.00	$77.00	$74.00	$74.00	$73.50
KCO	King Cola	$53.00	$60.00	$60.00	$62.50	$62.50	$61.00	$61.00	$61.00
KRK	Kringle's	$43.00	$40.00	$40.00	$37.00	$37.00	$35.50	$35.50	$35.00
MON	Mooncent	$26.75	$25.00	$25.00	$23.00	$23.00	$20.75	$20.75	$20.00
PRTO	Perry Auto	$41.00	$36.00	$36.00	$37.50	$37.50	$40.00	$40.00	$42.00
PT	Pasture	$29.00	$25.00	$25.00	$24.00	$24.00	$26.00	$26.00	$27.25
QZT	Quizet	$52.00	$53.50	$53.50	$56.00	$56.00	$59.00	$59.00	$60.00
SES	Seven Stars	$6.00	$6.25	$6.25	$6.00	$6.00	$7.00	$7.00	$8.50
SHD	SchoolDays	$36.50	$39.50	$39.50	$44.00	$44.00	$46.00	$46.00	$47.00
SNK	Sneakerz	$60.00	$55.00	$55.00	$56.50	$56.50	$54.50	$54.50	$54.00
SPD	Speed Demon	$111.75	$120.00	$120.00	$122.00	$122.00	$125.00	$125.00	$126.00
SRP	Slurp Soups	$39.25	$36.00	$36.00	$35.50	$35.50	$36.50	$36.50	$36.75
WTW	Walt World	$34.50	$34.50	$34.50	$36.75	$36.75	$37.25	$37.25	$38.35

Mathematics in the Marketplace © Prufrock Press Inc.

85

Permission is granted to photocopy or reproduce this page for single classroom use only.

STOCK CERTIFICATES

....

Stock Certificate

On ___/___/___ _____ *Purchased* _____
　　　　Date　　　　Name of buyer　　　　　　　　Number of Shares

Shares of _____ *Stock*
　　　　　　　　　　Name of company

_____　　　_____
Stockbrocker　　　　　　　　　Customer

Stock Certificate

On ___/___/___ _____ *Purchased* _____
　　　　Date　　　　Name of buyer　　　　　　　　Number of Shares

Shares of _____ *Stock*
　　　　　　　　　　Name of company

_____　　　_____
Stockbrocker　　　　　　　　　Customer

Stock Certificate

On ___/___/___ _____ *Purchased* _____
　　　　Date　　　　Name of buyer　　　　　　　　Number of Shares

Shares of _____ *Stock*
　　　　　　　　　　Name of company

_____　　　_____
Stockbrocker　　　　　　　　　Customer

Lesson 6

Concepts

- Graphs
- Charts
- Preparing presentations

Materials

- Investor rubric (p. 90)
- Banker rubric (p. 91)
- Stockbroker rubric (p. 92)
- Final presentation guide (p. 93)

Student Objective

The student utilizes data to create graphs and charts that document his or her experiences as a banker, stockbroker, or investor.

Introduction

If possible, make arrangements for your class to have access to a computer lab. Review the appropriate rubrics (and the final presentation guide provided, if you wish) with students, distributing them so that students are aware of the criteria by which they will be judged. You can elect to have students read these aloud with you and give examples. Depending on what presentation method you have chosen for your class, explain to students what process they will use to present their results.

- **Fair model:** Students set up their presentations in an assigned location. The teacher and any visitors circulate, ask questions, and use the provided rubric to assess the students' work.
- **Class presentation:** Each bank, brokerage house, and individual investor makes a presentation to the class while the teacher assesses the student's work using the rubric.

Recognition

Students give examples of the behaviors described by the rubric, and then they plan their posters for the fair or presentation in accordance with the elements explained by the rubric.

Application

Students compile their data and organize it in preparation for assessment.

1. Students reconcile their bank accounts and/or stock portfolios to generate data for their presentations.
2. Students use the data to create graphs, charts, posters, and so forth that demonstrate the decisions they made and the consequences of their choices.

Problem Solving

Using the rubrics provided, students analyze their records to document their successes.

3. Students construct visual aids and graphs.
4. Students write their findings in report or letter format.
5. Students prepare appropriate daily reports, reflections, and applied strategies paragraphs for submission.

Grade-Level Expectations

The student:

*   Organizes and displays data using tables, line graphs, or stem-and-leaf plots to answer questions related to the data, to analyze the data, to formulate or justify conclusions, to make predictions, or to solve problems.
*   Analyzes patterns, trends, or distributions in data in a variety of contexts by determining or using measures of central tendency or dispersion to analyze situations or solve problems.
*   Creates and uses representations to communicate mathematical ideas and to solve problems.
*   Uses models and technology to develop equivalent representations of the same mathematical concept.
*   Uses and creates representations to solve problems and organize his or her thoughts and ideas.
*   Is able to convert between representations.

Additional Notes

- If possible, we recommend that you schedule time in a computer lab so that students have access to computer programs as they design their presentations. This will allow their presentations to be more organized and professional.
- It is up to you what requirements to set in place for the final presentation. You might decide to have students dress for their roles, to mandate a portfolio, and so forth. We have provided a handout that has proved useful for us.

INVESTOR RUBRIC

	EXPERT	PROFICIENT	EMERGING	INCOMPLETE
SUPPORT FOR CONCLUSIONS	Investor chooses most financially sound stocks. Investor offers both mathematical and logical support for the conclusions drawn. Investor provides evidence that would convince the grandparents he or she is able to invest money.	Investor chooses financially sound stocks. Investor offers mathematical support for the conclusions drawn, but fails to make logical connections that may have led to more appropriate choices.	Investor chooses one of three most appropriate stocks but offers no support for this choice, or chooses one of the least appropriate stocks and offers inappropriate support for the choice.	Investor bases decisions on a guess or is unable to reach a decision.
STRATEGY AND CALCULATIONS	Investor analyzes the problem using multiplicative logic to demonstrate rate of change, percent increase/decrease, and so on for past stock performances. Investor chooses an appropriate strategy for calculating, estimating, and predicting.	Investor analyzes the problem using additive logic to demonstrate the rate of change for past stock performances. Investor chooses an appropriate strategy for calculating, estimating, and predicting.	Investor uses neither additive nor multiplicative logic to analyze past stock performances. Investor chooses an inappropriate strategy or misapplies an appropriate strategy.	Investor begins the process of logical and mathematical applications to solve the problem, but does not complete calculations or make appropriate estimations.
SUPPORTING MATERIALS	Investor's calculations and/or graphs are mathematically accurate. Calculations, estimations, and graphs clearly support the decisions made and work in concert with the logic of the chosen strategy.	Calculations and/or graphs are mathematically accurate with the exception of minor errors in calculations, estimations, predictions, or graphs that neither interfere with nor affect the decision.	Calculations and/or graphs are inaccurate. Errors interfere with the decision, or no clear connection exists between the decision and the calculations, estimations, predictions, or graphs.	Investor makes no calculations or graphs, or many or major errors prevent him or her from solving the problem.
JUSTIFICATION	Problem-solving process is clearly described so that anyone reading the discussion could reproduce the process and understand the decisions made.	Problem-solving process is clear enough so that someone reading the discussion could glean a basic understanding of how decisions were made, but he or she may have a few questions.	There is little evidence of how decisions were made. The problem-solving process is not reproducible by a reader.	Investor leaves no evidence of how decisions were reached, or he or she indicates that decisions were made by guessing, indicating no logical or mathematical underpinnings to support the guesses.
PRESENTATION	Writing is legible and neat, and graphs are easy to understand. Response has a professional quality. Investor uses correct grammar and spelling.	Writing and graphs are legible. Investor makes minor errors in grammar and/or spelling that do not distract the reader.	Writing and graphs are difficult to follow. Errors in grammar and/or spelling interfere with the reader's understanding.	Investor's response is presented in note form or is unprofessional, and there is little to no flow from one idea to the next. The reader cannot decipher graphs and/or sentences.

These rubrics were based on the work of Drs. Moon, Brighton, Callahan, and Tomlinson under the Educational and Research Centers PR/Award Number R206R50001. All rights permission secured.

BANKER RUBRIC

	EXPERT	PROFICIENT	EMERGING	INCOMPLETE
SUPPORT FOR CONCLUSIONS	Banker identifies patterns in customer behavior. Banker offers both mathematical and logical support for the conclusions drawn from these patterns. Using these conclusions, he or she makes recommendations for future customers.	Banker identifies patterns in customer behavior. Banker offers mathematical support for the conclusions drawn, but fails to make logical connections that impact recommendations.	Banker identifies some patterns of behavior but offers no support for the choice, or he or she offers support but never states observed patterns.	Banker is unable to identify patterns or the absence of patterns and offers no recommendations.
STRATEGY AND CALCULATIONS	Banker analyzes the problem using multiplicative logic to demonstrate rate of change, percent increase/decrease, and patterns of use. Banker chooses an appropriate strategy for calculating, estimating, and predicting.	Banker analyzes the problem using additive logic to demonstrate the rate of change and patterns of use. Banker chooses an appropriate strategy for calculating, estimating, and predicting.	Banker uses neither additive nor multiplicative logic to analyze customer use. Banker chooses an inappropriate strategy or misapplies an appropriate strategy.	Banker begins the process of logical and mathematical applications to solve the problem, but does not complete calculations or make appropriate estimations.
SUPPORTING MATERIALS	Calculations and/or graphs are mathematically accurate. Calculations, estimations, and graphs clearly support the decisions made and work in concert with the logic of the chosen strategy.	Calculations and/or graphs are mathematically accurate with the exception of minor errors in calculations, estimations, predictions, or graphs that neither interfere with nor affect the decision.	Calculations and/or graphs are inaccurate. Errors interfere with the decision, or no clear connection exists between the decision and the calculations, estimations, predictions, or graphs.	Banker makes no calculations or graphs, or many and/or major errors prevent him or her from solving the problem.
JUSTIFICATION	Problem-solving process is clearly described so that anyone reading the discussion could reproduce the process and understand the conclusions made.	Problem-solving process is clear enough that someone reading the discussion could glean a basic understanding of how decisions were made, but he or she may have a few questions.	There is little evidence of how decisions were made. The problem-solving process is not reproducible by a reader.	Banker leaves no evidence of how decisions were reached, or he or she indicates that the decision was based on a guess, indicating no logical or mathematical underpinnings to support the guess.
PRESENTATION	Writing is legible and neat and graphs are easy to understand. Response has a professional quality. Banker uses correct grammar and spelling.	Writing and graphs are legible. Banker makes minor errors in grammar and/or spelling that do not distract the reader.	Writing and graphs are difficult to follow. Errors in grammar and/or spelling interfere with the reader's understanding.	Response is presented in note form, and there is little to no flow from one idea to the next. Reader cannot decipher graphs and/or sentences.

These rubrics were based on the work of Drs. Moon, Brighton, Callahan, and Tomlinson under the Educational and Research Centers PR/Award Number R206R50001. All rights permission secured.

STOCKBROKER RUBRIC

	EXPERT	PROFICIENT	EMERGING	INCOMPLETE
SUPPORT FOR CONCLUSIONS	Broker chooses most financially sound stocks. Broker offers both mathematical and logical support for the conclusions drawn. Broker provides evidence that would convince investors that he or she is trustworthy.	Broker chooses financially sound stocks. Broker offers mathematical support for the conclusions drawn, but fails to make logical connections that may have led to more appropriate choices.	Broker chooses one of three most appropriate stocks but offers no support for this choice, or chooses one of the least appropriate stocks and offers inappropriate support for the choice.	Broker bases decisions on a guess or is unable to reach a decision.
STRATEGY AND CALCULATIONS	Broker analyzes the problem using multiplicative logic to demonstrate rate of change, percent increase/decrease, and so on for past stock performances. Broker chooses an appropriate strategy for calculating, estimating, and predicting.	Broker analyzes the problem using additive logic to demonstrate the rate of change for past stock performances. Broker chooses an appropriate strategy for calculating, estimating, and predicting.	Broker uses neither additive nor multiplicative logic to analyze past stock performances. Broker chooses an inappropriate strategy or misapplies an appropriate strategy.	Broker begins the process of logical and mathematical applications to solve the problem, but does not complete calculations or make appropriate estimations.
SUPPORTING MATERIALS	Broker's calculations and/or graphs are mathematically accurate. Calculations, estimations, and graphs clearly support the decisions made and work in concert with the logic of the chosen strategy.	Calculations and/or graphs are mathematically accurate with the exception of minor errors in calculations, estimations, predictions, or graphs that neither interfere with nor affect the decision.	Calculations and/or graphs are inaccurate. Errors interfere with the decision, or no clear connection exists between the decision and the calculations, estimations, predictions, or graphs.	Broker makes no calculations or graphs, or many or major errors prevent him or her from solving the problem.
JUSTIFICATION	The problem-solving process is clearly described so that anyone reading the discussion could reproduce the process and understand the decisions made.	The problem-solving process is clear enough so that someone reading the discussion could glean a basic understanding of how decisions were made, but he or she may have a few questions.	There is little evidence of how decisions were made. The problem-solving process is not reproducible by a reader.	Broker leaves no evidence of how decisions were reached, or he or she indicates that decisions were made by guessing, indicating no logical or mathematical underpinnings to support the guesses.
PRESENTATION	Writing is legible and neat, and graphs are easy to understand. Response has a professional quality. Broker uses correct grammar and spelling.	Writing and graphs are legible. Broker makes minor errors in grammar and/or spelling that do not distract the reader.	Writing and graphs are difficult to follow. Errors in grammar and/or spelling interfere with the reader's understanding.	Broker's response is presented in note form or is unprofessional, and there is little to no flow from one idea to the next. The reader cannot decipher graphs and/or sentences.

These rubrics were based on the work of Drs. Moon, Brighton, Callahan, and Tomlinson under the Educational and Research Centers PR/Award Number R206R50001. All rights permission secured.

FINAL PRESENTATION GUIDE

Bankers

- Dress the part of a banker.
- Complete all worksheets, and rewrite them to be legible if necessary.
- Create an attractive poster (either flat or trifold) displaying the following:
  - o   your bank name and logo,
  - o   a broken-line-graph that shows daily gains and losses,
  - o   a one- or two-paragraph summary explaining what strategies you used to service your customers, and
  - o   a one- or two-paragraph reflection on your experience as a banker.

Stockbrokers

- Dress the part of a stockbroker.
- Complete all worksheets, and rewrite them to be legible if necessary.
- Create an attractive poster (either flat or trifold) displaying the following:
  - o   your brokerage house's name and logo,
  - o   a broken-line-graph that shows daily gains and losses,
  - o   a one- or two-paragraph summary explaining what strategies you used to service your customers, and
  - o   a one- or two-paragraph reflection on your experience as a stockbroker.

Investors

- Dress professionally.
- Complete all worksheets, and rewrite them to be legible if necessary.
- Create an attractive poster (either flat or trifold) displaying the following:
  - o   the stocks that you purchased,
  - o   a broken-line-graph that shows daily gains and losses,
  - o   a one- or two-paragraph summary explaining what strategies you used to determine your investment decisions, and
  - o   a one- or two-paragraph reflection on your experience as an investor.

Lesson 7

Concepts

- Authentic performance assessment
- Student self-evaluation

Materials

- Presentation schedule (p. 97)
- Self-Evaluation sheet (p. 98)
- Response cards (pp. 99)
- Student Reflection sheet (p. 100)
- Voting ballots (pp. 101–102)
- Stock Market Posttest sheet (p. 103)
- Stock market pretest/posttest answer key (p. 20)

Student Objective

The student self-evaluates his or her performance, shares work, and reflects on the unit.

Introduction

Begin class by reviewing the rubric(s) one final time.

Recognition

Students assess their own work using the Self-Evaluation sheet.

Application

According to the presentation style you have chosen, make the necessary preparations and have students demonstrate what they have learned.

1. For the fair model, have students set up their presentations in the assigned location. The teacher and any visitors should circulate, asking questions to check for student understanding and making assessments according to the rubric. Rounds can be held during which one group (e.g., bankers) is allowed to circulate and view the presentations of other students (e.g., investors and stockbrokers). Repeat these rounds until all students have had the opportunity to see everybody else's work.

2. For the presentation model, have students sign up for a presentation time and date. Teachers, any visitors, and other students watch each presentation, asking questions (either throughout or at the close of the presentation) to check for understanding. For each presentation, audience members should fill out the response cards provided.

Problem Solving

Students should reflect on their own and others' experiences in the simulation.

1. Have students review the response cards generated for their presentations and their Self-Evaluation sheets, along with the completed rubrics, if you so choose.

2. Have students complete the Student Reflection sheet.

3. Have students vote for which student performed best in each of the three roles.

4. Distribute the posttest and have students complete it.

Grade-Level Expectations

The student:

- Organizes and displays data using tables, line graphs, or stem-and-leaf plots to answer questions related to the data, to analyze the data, to formulate or justify conclusions, to make predictions, or to solve problems.
- Analyzes patterns, trends, or distributions in data in a variety of contexts by determining or using measures of central tendency or dispersion to analyze situations or solve problems.
- Creates and uses representations to communicate mathematical ideas and to solve problems.
- Uses models and technology to develop equivalent representations of the same mathematical concept.
- Uses and creates representations to solve problems and to organize thoughts and ideas.
- Is able to convert between representations.

Additional Notes

- In our experience, it is helpful to invite fellow teachers, parents, and administrators to attend the fair and to serve as judges. Observations and results submitted by visitors are helpful, as you will be busy observing all of your students, and occasionally, they notice things that you might miss.
- If you are providing students with grades, use your observations of students from the simulation days, your and other judges' opinions of the final presentation, and the degree of student improvement (as observed and as shown by the pretest and posttest) to assign grades.

PRESENTATION SCHEDULE

	Name	**Time**
1.		
2.		
3.		
4.		
5.		
6.		
7.		
8.		
9.		
10.		
11.		
12.		
13.		
14.		
15.		
16.		
17.		
18.		
19.		
20.		

Name:_____ Date: _____

SELF-EVALUATION

In this unit, I played the role of a(n) _____.

1. I have provided evidence of the following mathematical processes in my presentation for the unit (circle all that apply):

    Addition and subtraction

    Multiplication

    Percentages

    Return on investment (ROI)

2. My charts and/or my graphs clearly show the following:_____

    _____

    _____

    _____

3. During this unit, I reached the following conclusions:_____

    _____

    _____

    _____

4. My visual aid(s) and written work is (circle all that apply):

    Neat

    Eye-catching

    Proofread and checked

RESPONSE CARDS

Presenter's name: _____

Your name: _____

Positive criticism:	Constructive criticism:

Presenter's name: _____

Your name: _____

Positive criticism:	Constructive criticism:

Name:_____ Date: _____

STUDENT REFLECTION

After reading through people's evaluations of my presentation and considering my own self-evaluation, I think . . ._____

_____

_____

_____

_____

_____

_____

_____

I did really well with . . . _____

_____

_____

_____

_____

_____

_____

If I could do it again, I would try to improve by . . ._____

_____

_____

_____

_____

_____

VOTE FOR THE BEST STOCKBROKER

Consider the following issues as you make your choice:
- Were this stockbroker's calculations accurate?
- Did this stockbroker explain his or her strategies clearly?
- Did this stockbroker's customers make good returns on their investments?

To vote for your choice, write the stockbroker's name below.

I vote for: _____

VOTE FOR THE BEST BANKER

Consider the following issues as you make your choice:
- Were this banker's calculations accurate?
- Did this banker explain his or her recommendations clearly?
- Were this banker's customers happy with the services that he or she provided?

To vote for your choice, write the banker's name below.

I vote for: _____

VOTE FOR THE BEST INVESTORS

Consider the following issues as you make your choice:
- Did these investors use all of the available resources and make sound choices as a result?
- Did these investors clearly explain their strategies?
- Did these investors make good rates of return on investments?

To vote for your choice, write three investors' names below.

I vote for:

_____

_____

_____

STOCK MARKET POSTTEST

Please complete the following multiple-choice questions to the best of your ability. This test is intended to measure what you have learned during this unit.

1. A stock is:
    A. a type of racing car
    B. a share of a company
    C. a savings option at the bank
    D. make-believe money

2. A stock market table helps you to:
    A. calculate your earnings or losses on stock
    B. know how many shares of a company's stock were sold in a day
    C. use the stock ticker symbol for various companies
    D. all of the above

3. Which of the following statements is true when you are investing money?
    A. "The larger risk you take, the less you earn."
    B. "Risk has nothing to do with the amount you stand to earn from an investment."
    C. "The riskier the investment, the higher the gain if the risk is successful."
    D. "Safer investments yield the highest returns on your investment."

4. In calculating the return on your investment (ROI), you must:
    A. add the money you spent and the money you earned (ROI = R + I)
    B. divide your investment by your return (ROI = I / R)
    C. subtract your investment from your return and divide by the investment (ROI = (R – I) / I)
    D. add your investment to your return and divide by 52 (ROI = (I + R) / 52)

5. In order to convert your ROI to a percentage, you must:
    A. multiply by 100
    B. add 1/100
    C. divide by 10
    D. add 100

6. How would you rate yourself in terms of risk taking?
   A. I am very comfortable taking risks.
   B. Sometimes I take risks.
   C. It makes me very nervous to take risks.
   D. I avoid taking risks at all costs.

7. If you buy 10 shares at $20 a share, and you have $208 at the end of the week, then what was the return on your investment? State it as a percentage. Please show your work!

8. If you deposit $400 in the bank in a saving account that yields 5% interest a year, how much will your account have earned after 12 months? Please show your work!

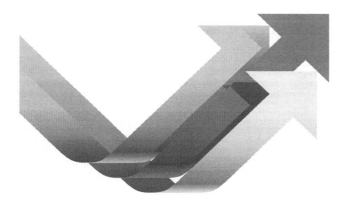

Appendix
Student Context Rubric

The Student Context Rubric (SCR) is intended for use by the classroom teacher as a tool to help in the identification of students of masked potential. This term, *masked potential*, refers to students who are gifted, but are frequently not identified because their behaviors are not displayed to best advantage by traditional methods. The SCR was designed to be used with this series of units and the authentic performance assessments that accompany them. Although you may choose to run the units without using the SCR, you may find the rubric helpful for keeping records of student behaviors.

The units serve as platforms for the display of student behaviors, while the SCR is an instrument that teachers can use to record those behaviors when making observations. The rubric requires the observer to record the frequency of gifted behaviors, but there is also the option to note that the student demonstrates the behavior with particular intensity. In this way, the rubric is subjective and requires careful observation and consideration.

It is recommended that an SCR be completed for each student prior to the application of a unit, and once again upon completion of the unit. In this way, teachers will be reminded of behaviors to look for during the unit—particularly those behaviors that we call *loophole behaviors*, which may indicate giftedness but are often misinterpreted or overlooked. (For instance, a student's verbal ability can be missed if he or she uses it to spin wild lies about having neglected to complete an assignment.) Therefore, the SCR allows teachers to be aware of—and to document—high-ability behavior even if it is masked or used in nontraditional ways. The mechanism also provides a method for tracking changes in teachers' perceptions of their students, not only while students are working on the Interactive Discovery-Based Units for High-Ability Learners, but also while they are engaged in traditional classroom activities.

In observing student behaviors, you might consider some of the following questions after completing a lesson:

- Was there anyone or anything that surprised you today?
- Did a particular student jump out at you today?
- Did someone come up with a unique or unusual idea today?
- Was there a moment in class today when you saw a lightbulb go on? Did it involve an individual, a small group, or the class as a whole?
- In reviewing written responses after a class discussion, were you surprised by anyone (either because he or she was quiet during the discussion but had good written ideas, or because he or she was passionate in the discussion but did not write with the same passion)?
- Did any interpersonal issues affect the classroom today? If so, how were these issues resolved?
- Did the lesson go as planned today? Were there any detours?
- Is there a student whom you find yourself thinking or worrying about outside of school?
- Are there students in your classroom who seem to be on a rollercoaster of learning—"on" one day, but "off" the next?
- Are your students different outside of the classroom? In what ways are they different?
- Are there students who refuse to engage with the project?
- During a class performance, did the leadership of a group change when students got in front of their peers?
- Did your students generate new ideas today?
- What was the energy like in your class today? Did you provide the energy, or did the students?
- How long did it take the students to engage today?

Ideally, multiple observers complete the SCR for each student. If a gifted and talented specialist is available, we recommend that he or she assist. By checking off the appropriate marks to describe student behaviors, and by completing the scoring chart, participants generate quantifiable data that can be used in advocating for students who would benefit from scaffolded services. **In terms of students' scores on the SCR, we do not provide concrete cutoffs or point requirements regarding which students should be recommended for special services.** Rather, the SCR is intended to flag students for scaffolded services and to enable them to reach their potential. It also provides a way to monitor and record students' behaviors.

What follows is an explanation of the categories and items included on the SCR, along with some examples of how the specified student behaviors might be evidenced in your classroom.

Engagement

1. **Student arrives in class with new ideas to bring to the project that he or she has thought of outside of class.** New ideas may manifest themselves as ideas about how to approach a problem, about new research information found on the Internet or elsewhere outside of class, about something in the news or in the paper that is relevant to the subject, or about a connection between the subject and an observed behavior.

2. **Student shares ideas with a small group of peers, but may fade into the background in front of a larger group.** The student may rise to be a leader when the small group is working on a project, but if asked to get up in front of the class, then that student fades into the background and lets others do the talking.

3. **Student engagement results in a marked increase in the quality of his or her performance.** This is particularly evident in a student who does not normally engage in class at all. During the unit, the student suddenly becomes engaged and produces something amazing.

4. **Student eagerly interacts with appropriate questions, but may be reluctant to put things down on paper.** This is an example of a loophole behavior, or one that causes a student to be overlooked when teachers and specialists are identifying giftedness. It is particularly evident in students who live in largely "oral" worlds, which is to say that they communicate best verbally and are often frustrated by written methods, or in those who have writing disabilities.

Creativity

1. **Student intuitively makes "leaps" in his or her thinking.** Occasionally, you will be explaining something, and a lightbulb will go on for a student, causing him or her to take the concept far beyond the content being covered. Although there are students who do this with regularity, it is more often an intensity behavior, meaning that when it occurs, the student is very intense in his or her thinking, creativity, reasoning, and so on. This can be tricky to identify, because often, the student is unable to explain his or her thinking, and the teacher realizes only later that a leap in understanding was achieved.

2. **Student makes up new rules, words, or protocols to express his or her own ideas.** This can take various forms, one of which is a student's taking two words and literally combining them to try to express what he or she is thinking about. Other times, a student will want to change the rules to make his or her idea possible.

3. **Student thinks on his or her feet in response to a project challenge, to make excuses, or to extend his or her work.** This is another loophole

behavior, because it often occurs when a student is being defensive or even misbehaving, making a teacher less likely to interpret it as evidence of giftedness. It is sometimes on display during classroom debates and discussions.

4. **Student uses pictures or other inventive means to illustrate his or her ideas.** Given the choice, this student would rather draw an idea than put it into words. This could take the shape of the student creating a character web or a design idea. The student might also act out an idea or use objects to demonstrate understanding.

Synthesis

1. **Student goes above and beyond directions to expand ideas.** It is wonderful to behold this behavior in students, particularly when displayed by those students who are rarely engaged. A student may be excited about a given idea and keep generating increasingly creative or complex material to expand upon that idea. For instance, we had a student who, during the mock trial unit, became intrigued by forensic evidence and decided to generate and interpret evidence to bolster his team's case.

2. **Student has strong opinions on projects, but may struggle to accept directions that contradict his or her opinions.** This student may understand directions, but be unwilling to yield to an idea that conflicts with his or her own idea. This behavior, rather than indicating a lack of understanding, is typical of students with strong ideas.

3. **Student is comfortable processing new ideas.** This behavior is evident in students who take new ideas and quickly extend them or ask insightful questions.

4. **Student blends new and old ideas.** This behavior has to do with processing a new idea, retrieving an older idea, and relating the two to one another. For instance, a student who learns about using string to measure distance might remember making a treasure map and extrapolate that a string would have been useful for taking into account curves and winding paths.

Interpersonal Ability

1. **Student is an academic leader who, when engaged, increases his or her levels of investment and enthusiasm in the group.** This is a student who has so much enthusiasm for learning that he or she makes the project engaging for the whole group, fostering an attitude of motivation or optimism.

2. **Student is a social leader in the classroom, but may not be an academic leader.** To observe this type of behavior, you may have to be vigilant, for some students are disengaged in the classroom but come alive as soon as they cross the threshold into the hallway, where they can socialize with their

peers. Often, this student is able to get the rest of the group to do whatever he or she wants (and does not necessarily use this talent for good).

3. **Student works through group conflict to enable the group to complete its work.** When the group has a conflict, this is the student who solves the problem or addresses the issue so that the group can get back to work. This is an interpersonal measure, and thus, it does not describe a student who simply elects to do all of the work rather than confronting his or her peers about sharing the load.

4. **Student is a Tom Sawyer in classroom situations, using his or her charm to get others to do the work.** There is an important distinction to watch out for when identifying this type of behavior: You must be sure that the student is *not* a bully, coercing others to do his or her work. Instead, this student actually makes other students *want* to lend a helping hand. For instance, a twice-exceptional student who is highly talented but struggles with reading might develop charm in order to get other students to transpose his verbally expressed ideas into writing.

Verbal Communication

1. **Participation in brainstorming sessions (e.g., group work) increases student's productivity.** When this type of student is given the opportunity to verbally process with peers, he or she is often able to come up with the answer. For instance, if asked outright for an answer, this student may shrug, but if given a minute to consult with a neighbor, then the student usually is able and willing to offer the correct answer.

2. **Student constructively disagrees with peers and/or the teacher by clearly sharing his or her thoughts.** This student can defend his or her point of view with examples and reasoning—not just in a formal debate, but also in general classroom situations. He or she has learned to channel thoughts into constructive disagreement, rather than flying off the handle merely to win an argument.

3. **Student verbally expresses his or her academic and/or social needs.** This student can speak up when confused or experiencing personality clashes within a group. This student knows when to ask for help and can clearly articulate what help is needed.

4. **Student uses strong word choice and a variety of tones to bring expression to his or her verbal communication.** This student is an engaging speaker and speaks loudly and clearly enough for everybody to hear. A wide vocabulary is also indicative that this student's verbal capability is exceptional.

Student: _____

Date: _____

Fill out the rubric according to what you have observed about each student's behaviors. Then, for each area, record the number of items you marked "Not observed," "Sometimes," and "Often." Multiply these tallies by the corresponding point values (0, 1, and 2) to get the totals for each area. There is an option to check for high intensity so you can better keep track of students' behaviors.

ENGAGEMENT

1. Student arrives in class with new ideas to bring to the project that he or she has thought of outside of class.
   Not observed　　Sometimes　　Often　　High intensity

2. Student shares ideas with a small group of peers, but may fade into the background in front of a larger group.
   Not observed　　Sometimes　　Often　　High intensity

3. Student engagement results in a marked increase in the quality of his or her performance.
   Not observed　　Sometimes　　Often　　High intensity

4. Student eagerly interacts with appropriate questions, but may be reluctant to put things down on paper.
   Not observed　　Sometimes　　Often　　High intensity

CREATIVITY

1. Student intuitively makes "leaps" in his or her thinking.
   Not observed　　Sometimes　　Often　　High intensity

2. Student makes up new rules, words, or protocols to express his or her own ideas.
   Not observed　　Sometimes　　Often　　High intensity

3. Student thinks on his or her feet in response to a project challenge, to make excuses, or to extend his or her work.
   Not observed　　Sometimes　　Often　　High intensity

4. Student uses pictures or other inventive means to illustrate his or her ideas.
   Not observed　　Sometimes　　Often　　High intensity

SYNTHESIS

1. Student goes above and beyond directions to expand ideas.
   Not observed　　Sometimes　　Often　　High intensity

2. Student has strong opinions on projects, but may struggle to accept directions that contradict his or her opinions.
   Not observed　　Sometimes　　Often　　High intensity

3. Student is comfortable processing new ideas.
   Not observed　　Sometimes　　Often　　High intensity

4. Student blends new ideas and old ideas.
   Not observed　　Sometimes　　Often　　High intensity

INTERPERSONAL ABILITY

1. Student is an academic leader who, when engaged, increases his or her levels of investment and enthusiasm in the group.
   Not observed　　Sometimes　　Often　　High intensity

2. Student is a social leader in the classroom, but may not be an academic leader.
   Not observed　　Sometimes　　Often　　High intensity

3. Student works through group conflict to enable the group to complete its work.
   Not observed　　Sometimes　　Often　　High intensity

4. Student is a Tom Sawyer in classroom situations, using his or her charm to get others to do the work.
   Not observed　　Sometimes　　Often　　High intensity

VERBAL COMMUNICATION

1. Participation in brainstorming sessions (e.g., group work) increases student's productivity.
   Not observed　　Sometimes　　Often　　High intensity

2. Student constructively disagrees with peers and/or the teacher by clearly sharing his or her thoughts.
   Not observed　　Sometimes　　Often　　High intensity

3. Student verbally expresses his or her academic and/or social needs.
   Not observed　　Sometimes　　Often　　High intensity

4. Student uses strong word choice and a variety of tones to bring expression to his or her verbal communication.
   Not observed　　Sometimes　　Often　　High intensity

AREA	NOT 0	SOME 1	OFTEN 2	HIGH	TOTAL
ENGAGEMENT					
CREATIVITY					
SYNTHESIS					
INTERPERSONAL ABILITY					
VERBAL COMMUNICATION					
ADD TOTALS					

STUDENT CONTEXT RUBRIC

Developed by Cote & Blauvelt under the auspices of the Further Steps Forward Project, a Jacob Javits grant program, #S206A050086.

Mathematics in the Marketplace © Prufrock Press Inc.

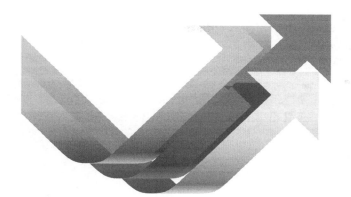

About the Authors

Richard G. Cote, M.B.A., is a career educator. He has dedicated 41 years to being a classroom teacher (mathematics, physics), a community college adjunct instructor (economics), a gifted and talented resource specialist, and the director of the Further Steps Forward Project, funded under Javits legislation.

His development of the MESH (mathematics, English, science, and history) program has led him to several audiences. He has presented at various national conventions, civic/community groups, district school boards, teacher organizations, community colleges, and universities and has served as a consultant to educators throughout the country. Cote helped develop the teacher certification examination for physics at the Institute for Educational Testing and Research at the University of South Florida. He completed the Florida Council on Educational Management Program in Educational Leadership, and he is the recipient of numerous awards, including a certificate of merit on economics education from the University of South Florida, a grant from the Florida Council on Economics Education, a Florida Compact award, and a prestigious NAGC Curriculum Studies award for the development of *Ecopolis* and *What's Your Opinion?*

Now retired from the workplace, Cote continues to share his energy, creativity, and expertise with educators through the Interactive Discovery-Based Units for High-Ability Learners.

Darcy O. Blauvelt has been teaching in a variety of facilities for more than 12 years. Her educational journey has included public schools, private schools, nursery schools, and a professional theatre for children ages 3–18. Blauvelt holds educational certification in Theatre K–12, Early Childhood Education, and English Education 5–12. She holds a B.A. in theatre from Chatham College, Pittsburgh, PA, and has done graduate work at Lesley University, MA in creative arts in learning, as well as at Millersville University, PA in psychology.

In 2005, she joined the Nashua School District as a gifted and talented resource specialist. Subsequently, she served full time as the program coordinator for the Further Steps Forward Project, a Javits Grant program, from 2005–2009. Blauvelt returned to the classroom in the fall of 2009 and currently teaches seventh-grade English in Nashua, NH. Blauvelt lives in Manchester, NH with her husband, two dogs, five cats, and the occasional son!